Sharing and Responding

Sharing and Responding

Peter Elbow
University of Massachusetts at Amherst

Pat Belanoff
State University of New York at Stony Brook

Random House

New York

First Edition
987654321
Copyright © 1989 by Peter Elbow and Pat Belanoff

ISBN: 0-394-38621-3
        0-394-38622-1

Manufactured in the United States of America

ACKNOWLEDGMENT

Page 10: Excerpt from Robert Penn Warren from
Writers at Work, Second Series, edited by Malcolm
Cowley. Copyright © 1963, by The Paris Review, Inc.
All rights reserved. Reprinted by permission of Viking
Penguin, Inc.

Preface

Students can give each other excellent feedback, but most of them need some help and instruction in learning to do so. In this booklet we have gathered together a rich sequence of suggestions for how students can share their writing with each other and give and receive useful responses.

These suggestions for sharing and responding were originally scattered throughout the larger textbook (*A Community of Writers,* published in conjunction with this booklet)—each textbook unit ending with specific suggestions for peer feedback. But then we ran into a structural dilemma. We realized that we wanted to invite flexibility in the sequencing of the units so that teachers could juggle or rearrange them freely. Yet we still felt that students should follow a particular sequence in learning the array of methods for sharing and responding (moving from safety to risk to build trust—and from easier to harder).

It finally struck us that we could gather all the sharing and responding techniques together so as to maintain the sequence. At first we planned it as the last section of the textbook, but then we realized we could make a separate pamphlet. Here then is a booklet that is closely tied to our textbook (with frequent keys in the textbook to different sections of the booklet). But the booklet is also completely independent, and thus suitable for teachers who use no textbook or some other textbook—that is, for any teacher who wants to help students respond to one another's writing.

Indeed we hope we may tempt some teachers to try peer responding who have been reluctant to do so—or who have had bad experiences with it. For there is usually something messy and potentially chaotic about using peer groups. One is always trying to shout one last direction while students are moving into pairs or groups and chairs are scraping and the hubbub of talk is taking over. *"Oh yes, and don't forget to . . ."*—but they don't hear. And one is always photocopying directions and suggestions for feedback at the last minute. Nothing will ever make the use of pairs and small groups tidy and quiet (and who would want to). But we find this booklet helpful as a way to have more material on paper for students to read about the complex feedback process (sometimes the night before): explanations, examples, principles.

There are more techniques here than a student or teacher could use regularly. The important principle is that students need to try them out before being in a suitable position to decide which kinds of responses are most helpful for a particular piece of writing (and audience and situation).

When we use these techniques for peer responding we sometimes use pairs and sometimes small groups. We sometimes shuffle groups, but more often we stick with stable pairs or groups so that students can build up trust. We tend to practice or illustrate each responding technique in the whole class on one or two sample texts before sending students off into pairs or groups—so as to address any confusions or questions they might have. In the introduction to the booklet we talk more about the principles for sharing and responding. And we have written a tiny Instructor's Manual for this booklet, which is available from Random House.

Peter Elbow
Pat Belanoff

Contents

Introduction

We talk in company, we write alone. Obviously the solitary dimension of writing has advantages: we don't need others in order to write. But the solitary dimension has drawbacks too: sometimes we lose track of our audience as we write, and sometimes we even get lonely. Therefore in this booklet we give extra emphasis to the *collaborative* and *social* dimension of writing.

It might seem odd to put all our suggestions for sharing and responding into a separate booklet instead of including them in the main book. We have done so because we want you to practice the activities in a special order—in the order we give them—whereas the units of the book may be juggled in different orders. Thus these responding activities are suitable for virtually *any* unit in the book, though we usually also make brief feedback suggestions in the units themselves

In short, we are being somewhat pushy about sequence when it comes to sharing and responding. We have found that it is crucial to start with sharing and then move on to nonjudgmental kinds of responding before opening up to full criticism. This means moving from safety to risk. The progression builds trust: trust in yourself and in the others you work with. You can't give good responses to writing or benefit from them except in a situation of trust.

We trust you will tolerate our pushiness here—be willing to learn the modes of responding we present and in the order we present them—if we make it clear that our *goal* is to move on fairly quickly and put *you* in charge of the feedback process. We want you, as writer, to be able to choose whatever kind of feedback you need—depending on the time and the piece of writing. Yet you can't really take charge of the feedback process if you haven't learned enough *kinds* of feedback to ask for. With this booklet we aim to teach you a rich and varied range of ways to get responses to your writing so you can then go on to take charge of the feedback process in the future. One of the main reasons why many people don't like getting feedback on their writing is that they don't know what to ask for and so end up helplessly putting themselves in the hands of readers.

By the way, don't assume that the later kinds of responding are necessarily better because they are later or harder to use. Some of the earliest—especially plain sharing—remain the best even though they are the easiest to use.

You should probably be able to try out all the kinds of responding we describe in, say, the first half of the semester. We summarize *all* the techniques in a final section that you can refer to when you are trying to decide what kind of feedback you might want on any particular occasion. We summarize them even more briefly inside the back cover of this booklet.

Among all the ways of giving feedback we describe in this section, there is a very good one we don't mention which you should also keep in mind. Simply *write a letter to the writer*. By making it a letter—taking a fresh sheet of paper, addressing him or her by name ("Dear ————"), and speaking in your own voice—you dignify the writing and dignify yourself. It often helps you think of particularly useful things to say and helps you naturally tailor your feedback to that person. We would appreciate it if you would try out this mode by writing *us* a letter (care of the publisher) telling us what helped you in our book and what got in the way—and any suggestions you have for revising.

The Need for All Three Audience Relationships

We've designed this booklet on a premise we see confirmed over and over in our own writing and teaching: writing improves most from a balance of *all three* audience situations.

1. Private writing. We benefit from private writing—no audience—because of the safety it provides. With that safety comes an invitation to take risks. We introduce you to private writing at the very beginning of the course in the form of freewriting. We discuss and explore private writing most thoroughly in Unit 6.

2. Sharing. It is common to give your writing to an audience and get no response; it is a helpful, empowering, and enjoyable process. Yet many students have never had this experience because they have written only in school and always gotten feedback, sometimes even a grade. (Imagine how well you'd *speak* if you were graded on everything you said.)

It turns out that we learn most about writing with our mouths and our ears. With our mouths we *feel* how our words and phrases and sentences work. With our ears we *hear* how our words sound—and also the words of others. What's nice is that this learning is *physical,* it occurs quickly *and without teaching.* When a word is wrong or a sentence doesn't work, you feel it in your mouth and hear it in your ear. Usually you stumble in your reading and almost automatically pause and say, "What I mean to say is . . ." and come up with an improvement. You learn without having to theorize or ponder about what is good and bad writing. And you learn without anyone's having to *tell* you what's wrong or what doesn't work. Sharing helps you develop a better ear and a better sense of voice and rhythm. These are the strongest foundations of good writing. Sharing is a way to celebrate and learn at the same time—and it's the quickest way to learn about writing.

Some people *hate* sharing their writing. As they read their words aloud, they cringe: "Yuck! These words are awful." But that reaction is usually because they've gotten so much criticism of their writing in the past that they can't hear their writing without also hearing criticism of it in their minds. (No wonder they hate writing.) If they practice sharing their writing in a supportive setting, this painful reaction will gradually subside—and they too will begin to experience the pleasure of reading for the sake of communicating, not for the sake of getting criticized.

Sharing (with no response) is also important as preparation for the third audience situation: getting responses. Until you learn to read your writing aloud without being nervous and self-conscious, you won't benefit from the responses readers give you: you won't hear them very well. Similarly until you learn to *listen* to the writing of others—without worrying what your reactions are or how to give feedback—you won't be able to give good responses. Worry keeps you from hearing their writing well enough. Sharing gives you crucial practice in reading and listening.

3. Responding. Finally, of course, we *do* need to find out how readers respond to our writing. And we need responses from various readers, not just from the one reader who happens to be teacher. Readers in the world are enormously different, so if we learn only one reader's responses, we haven't learned what we need.

The kind of feedback we get most often is judgment ("It's good here; it's bad there") and advice ("Here's how to improve the bad parts"). In this booklet we will help you work on this kind of feedback, but first we want to enlarge the *range of kinds* of responses you can get to writing. In particular we want to show you many ways to give *nonjudgmental* feedback: feedback that helps you see more clearly what you've written and tells you what got through to readers—but which doesn't try to tell you which parts are good and bad. Nonjudgmental feedback presents you with evidence of how readers experience your writing and lets *you* make up your mind what to think and do about it.

Options for Sharing and Responding

It's important to realize how wide a range of options you have for sharing and getting responses to your writing. You probably can't use them all consistently, but you should try to make sure you *try* them all to see which are most helpful for various situations.

Early or late drafts? You can get responses to early drafts or late drafts—indeed, it helps to discuss your thinking even *before* you have written at all. And don't forget that it's also helpful to get feedback on *final* drafts even though you cannot or will not do any more revising. Even though you won't work any more on this particular piece, you will learn about your writing and how readers read: long-range learning and celebration too.

Sharing out loud or on paper? You can read your piece out loud or give your readers copies for them to read silently. The process of reading out loud brings learning: you can feel strengths and weaknesses physically in your ear and mouth. You can tell about responses by watching your listeners. And reading out loud is more alive. But if your piece is very long or time is short, you will need to use paper. Paper copy gives readers more time to read closely—especially if the material is technical. It gives them more privacy. New technology makes it easier to make multiple copies—using copiers or computers—but don't forget about good old carbon paper. (Nevertheless, if readers cannot follow you in two out-loud renderings, the writing isn't clear enough: it's no good blaming it on "the material.")

Responding out loud or on paper? Both ways are valuable. Written responses are usually more careful, and the writer gets to take them home to ponder while revising. Spoken responses are easier and more casual to give; they are more sociable if there's a group, and it's interesting for responders to hear the response of others.

There's a way to combine *written and spoken* responding. First, have all group members give copies of their paper to everyone else. Then members go home, read all the papers, and take a few notes on each to record their responses and reactions. But additionally each member has responsibility for giving a *careful* written response to *one* paper. When the group meets for sharing responses, the person who wrote the careful feedback starts by reading what he wrote (and hands his or her written feedback to the writer), but the others also chime in and add responses on the basis of their reading and notes. This method is particularly useful if there isn't much time for group work or if the pieces of writing are somewhat long.

Pairs or groups? On the one hand, the more people the better: readers are so different and reading is such a subjective act that you really don't know much if you only know how one or two readers react. On the other hand, more readers takes more time, and you *can* learn a lot from one reader if she is a good one—someone who can really tell you in detail about what goes on in her head as she reads your words. Also it's easier to build up a relationship of good honesty, trust, and support between just two people. (If you know you are working on something important and you know you will want to get feedback at various stages, you may have to use your trusted readers sparingly—one or two at a time.)

By the way, you can get both the multiple perspectives of groups and the trust of and support of pairs: first get brief feedback from the group and then divide into pairs for fuller responses and discussion. Some people prefer the opposite order: start with pairs and then move on to groups.

New faces or same old faces? There is a temptation to keep changing pairs or group members for variety and new perspectives. But good sharing and responding depend heavily on safety and trust, so we tend to prefer working with the same person or group. Certain things can't occur till reader and writer have built up trust, and that takes longer than you might think.

Working in small groups

- If you read out loud, read twice and pause after each reading. At the end get people to jot a few notes about their reactions before anyone speaks so they are not too influenced by hearing what others say.

- Start off for a while with a "messy" system where everyone throws in bits of feedback helter-skelter—though make sure everyone makes some contribution. Then after a number of weeks when people get more comfortable with the process, get each person to give his whole set of responses at once—with no one else joining in. For the goal is to see your writing through the consciousness of one person and then another. You can't do that if everyone's response is all mixed together with everyone else's.

- Avoid all arguments whether between responders or between a responder and writer. Not only do arguments waste time, they usually make responders less willing to be honest. Most of all you usually *benefit* from having different points of view—left standing, not reconciled. Don't look for a "right answer" but for how your writing looks through different sets of eyes. When readers disagree, that just helps the writer realize that she gets to make up her own mind about what it all means.

Two Sample Papers for Illustrating Different Kinds of Feedback

AN ORANGE BASKETBALL GAME
A Student

Of course we're here an hour before the game starts. I don't mind, though. Now I can see all the other crazy Syracuse Orangemen basketball fans besides me! My brother and I sit down, taking the whole scene in. The Carrier Dome is a massive building with a white, balloon-like roof. It can hold a 100-yard football field, but today there is a blue curtain cutting the area into two parts. One half has vendors selling refreshments and Syracuse University paraphernalia. There is also a stage with two men singing, tables with important patrons clad in orange, and a giant-sized screen which will show the game for the unfortunate fans sitting behind the blue curtain. On the other side of the blue curtain is the hard floor on which ten college men will bounce a one foot in diameter orange ball and attempt to throw it through a round metal loop with intertwined ropes hanging on it. This may not seem very difficult—shooting a ball through a hoop—but with rules to follow and five men trying to block your shot, it is not as easy as it appears. To add to the main attraction, the basketball court, on this side of the Dome, there are thousands of people milling about—all in orange, of course. These people are just like me, hoping that their team will have more points at the end of a forty minute game. These fans are tough. They have seen defeat many times, whether it was a blow-out the entire game or a last second luck shot causing a loss by one point. But they hope for the elation of winning. This feeling is what keeps them returning for more possible disappointments. The high is much higher than the low is low.

Finally it is ten minutes until the tip-off. People sit down and wait with extreme anticipation and excitement. I look around and see only one color—orange! Orange hats, t-shirts, sweatshirts, sweaters, pants, banners, scarfs, and even orange faces

6

everywhere. Free orange bandanas, passed out before the game, are waving in the air. The crowd is chanting, "Let's go Orange!" No one is sitting down now. On the court are ten college men, five on your side, five not. Those ten individuals have approximately 32,000 pairs of eyes on them. I think they might be a little nervous.

The ball is thrown up and a hush comes over the Dome—the game has begun. For two hours no one in that stadium will relax. The first shot is taken by Syracuse and it is also the first point of the game! Listening to the cheering for a moment, I hear different phrases. Some happy, enthusiastic, optimistic phrases such as, "Come on Orangemen, you can do it!" Other expressions were angry and pessimistic, "You guys stink! Get your act together!" Every fan believes that what he screams is heard by the players and helps them win the game. Every fan is a referee, too. "What? I saw that! It was a charge, not a defensive foul!" All these single voices blend together to create an unintelligible deafening roar. What a clamor!

The score is now tied with two minutes left in the first half. Two minutes in a basketball game is quite a long time. Everyone is anxious, wondering who will have the lead at half-time. The odors of hot dogs, mustard, sweat, beer, and stale air-conditioned ventilation combine as the temperature in the Carrier Dome rises. With thirty seconds to go, stocky pivot guard Pearl Washington of Syracuse dribbles the ball, intending to have the last shot of the first half. After what seems like a lifetime, with ten seconds left, he takes an outside shot and . . . it's good! Syracuse leads by two. Hysteria breaks out in the Dome.

During halftime, people try to carry on normal conversations but they always end up discussing the game. All age groups are present, from baby Orange fans with t-shirts reading, "Future Orangeman," to old businessmen with Orange sweaters and their own portable cushioned seats to place on the cold cement benches. With five minutes remaining until the second half, these loyal fans settle down to watch their team continue the game. Two questions are whirling in their brains, "What will happen this half? Will they win?"

I sit on the cement with my brother amid the orange sea and say with confidence, "Of course they will win!"

CLEANING UP THE ENVIRONMENT
Larry Kersh

I think it is disgusting the way people don't care about the environment they live in. I feel it is important for people to realize that the trash they throw on the ground is not going to be picked up. If everyone would make an effort to help clean the environment, then it would be much more appealing.

All people have to do is make an effort to find a garbage can to throw their trash into. They can even hold on to their trash until they get home where there is sure to be a trash receptacle. For example, I don't know how many times I've seen people throwing gum wrappers and cigarette butts on the ground when they are just a few feet away from a garbage can. I also remember a time when my brother and I went canoeing on the Delaware River. When it came time for lunch, we rowed over to one of the banks. As we pulled the canoe onto the bank, we noticed a pile of garbage near a deserted campsite. We both commented to each other about what we would like to do to these people if we caught them in the act. I suggested making them clear up an area of a certain radius. My brother suggested we make them eat it! There is definitely a need for people to become aware that others are not going to clean up their garbage. These above statements are of how things are outside the home environment. Now I would like to discuss the problems in the home (especially on campus). There are close to ten thousand students living here on campus. Nearly everyone has a roommate and must be considerate of others. In my suite, however, there is a problem. There have been times when I've come back to my room to find a pile of dishes in the bathroom, and all sorts of stuff in the suite room. My roommate is the major cause of these messes. He doesn't seem to realize that it bothers the rest of the people living here. He seems to take it for granted that we don't mind. If people don't see the damage caused by littering the home environment, or any environment, they are more apt to assume that the effects are very little, and therefore will continue their bad habit. It is so unfair to the people who are making an effort to clean up our environment.

Some of my opponents have argued that the cost of cleaning up the outside environment far outweighs the results that will come of it. These people must live in high-priced neighborhoods where their areas are clean, or they must dwell in places where they don't see trash all over the place. They are blind to the areas that need to be cleaned up. Others feel that no matter how much you do to clean the environment, it will still remain unclean and therefore all the money spent would be a waste. My suite mates have the opinion that it is a waste of time to clean up the suite because they feel that my roommate will just continue to make a mess. Although these are valid points, I feel that a clean environment is very important.

All of the people that are in favor of cleaning up their environment have a few options. They can raise money or donate it themselves. I am not asking all that are in favor to take responsibility for the ones that aren't in favor. I am asking for a little help from all of the concerned citizens to give a little of their time and effort.

In addition to these arguments for a cleaner environment, I would like to add that this would benefit animal life because they are unable to rid their environment of the trash left by human beings. I think that this issue should be discussed between legislatures and, more personally, my suite mates.

I

No Responding: Sharing

If you've never done freewriting before—writing words down and not show-ing them to anyone at all—it can feel peculiar. But quickly you find it nat-ural and helpful. Similarly if you've never done sharing before—reading your words to someone without getting any comments back at all—that too can feel peculiar. When you read your words out loud (or give a copy of your writing to someone) you probably have an urge to ask how the listeners *liked* it—whether they thought it was any *good*. Because all school writing is evaluated, we sometimes assume that the *point* of writing is to be evalu-ated. When we speak to people, do we immediately ask them how *good* our words were? No. We speak because we are trying to *communicate*. We cer-tainly don't expect listeners to give us a grade.

With sharing we're trying to emphasize writing as communicating rather than as performing for judgment. You'll find that it's a relief to give your writing to others (aloud or on paper) just to communicate, just for the fun of it—just so they can hear what you have to say and learn from you. It's a relief to say (on some occasions, anyway), "The hell with whether they liked it or not. I just want them to *hear* it." If you practice sharing in the right spirit, you will soon find it as natural and helpful as freewriting.

And what is the right spirit? In sharing, the goal is for writers to *give* and for listeners to *receive*. Writing is gift giving. When you give someone a gift, you don't want her to criticize; you want her to use it and enjoy it. If you happen to give someone a gift she doesn't like, do you want her to com-plain? No, you want her to thank you.

You will improve your writing much faster if you let us help you build a community in your classroom: a place where people hear clearly even

---

PROCESS BOX

> In the actual process of composition or in preliminary thinking, I try to immerse myself in the motive and *feel* toward meanings, rather than plan a structure or plan effects.
> ROBERT PENN WARREN, *PARIS REVIEW* INTERVIEW

---

what is mumbled, understand what is badly written, and look for the validity even in what they disagree with. *Eventually* you will learn to write to the enemy—to write surrounded by sharks. But you will learn that necessary skill better if, for a while, you practice writing to allies and listening to friends.

Sharing out loud and on paper. We stress reading your words out loud here, especially at first, because you learn so much by using your mouth and ears. And there is a special psychological benefit from learning to *say* your words out loud: you get over the fear of *making a noise* with your written words. But it is also useful to share silently, by giving readers a copy of what you've written. Periodically throughout the semester, please find occasions to make copies of what you've written and give them to others—just for the celebration of sharing.

Guidelines for Sharing Out Loud

To the writer:

- Take a moment to look at your listeners, relax, and take a deep breath. Say a few introductory words if necessary.

- Read slowly, clearly. Own your writing; read it with authority even if you are not satisfied with it.

- Concentrate on the meaning of what you're reading: don't worry about whether listeners like it.

- Take a pause between paragraphs.

- Let people interrupt to ask you to repeat or go slower, but don't let them give you any feedback.

- Read your piece a second time. Pause after the first reading but don't let people respond.

- When you are done, ask the group to go on to the next reader.

To the listeners:

- Your job is to receive without comment.
- If the writer is racing or mumbling so you can't understand, interrupt him—appreciatively but firmly—and say, "Wait a minute, go back, I couldn't hear. Please read more slowly and clearly."
- Get the writer to read twice. Don't refrain from being assertive.
- *Give no feedback of any kind.*
- Thank the writer and suggest that the next person read.

If everyone is sharing a piece on the same topic, you might agree to discuss the *topic* after everyone has read. But don't let the discussion turn into disguised feedback on each other's writing.

II

Descriptive Responding

A. Sayback
B. Pointing, Summarizing, What's Almost Said or Implied, Center of Gravity
C. Structure; Voice, Point of View, Attitude toward the Reader; Level of Abstraction or Concreteness; Language, Diction, Syntax
D. Metaphorical Descriptions

Why would anyone want feedback without criticism or advice?

1. We benefit from feedback on *early* drafts. When we put off feedback till after we've slaved over something, it's hard to revise because we've invested too much sweat and blood. Nonjudgmental or descriptive feedback lets us get early feedback (and new ideas) because it simply ignores the fact that, of course, there are obvious problems in our early draft. It makes readers into allies rather than adversaries while they help us *see* our still-evolving text better and give us new insights.

2. Perhaps we're trying out a kind of writing or an approach that we're weak at: we're trying to break out of the rut of what we can already do well. Or we're working on something so difficult but important that we don't want criticism yet. We need a reader to trust us, to trust that *we* can see faults ourselves and work through them. We just need some *perspective* on our piece. And frankly we also need some encouragement and support in seeing what's *right* or *strong* in the piece.

3. We may want feedback from a reader who is accurate and perceptive but she can do nothing except criticize. It's her only gear. We need her per-

ceptions but not her knife. These questions will help us nudge her out of her judgmental rut.

4. We often need to *give* feedback to a weak or inexperienced writer or to a writer in a rut. Often we sense that criticism and "helpful advice" are *not* what he needs. Sure, his writing has serious problems, but what he needs is encouragement and confidence. We often sense, in fact, that the very thing that's *undermining* his writing is too much criticism: he's clenching too hard. He's criticizing and rewriting every phrase as he writes it—until all the energy and clarity are gone from his writing. He's thinking about critics at every moment. He'll write better when he trusts himself better. Nonjudgmental feedback will help him do that.

IIA. DESCRIPTIVE RESPONDING: SAYBACK

Sayback (or active listening) is simple but subtle: the author reads and the listener "says back" what she hears: what she hears the writer is "getting at." But she says it back in a slightly open, questioning fashion in order to *invite the writer to restate* what she means. In effect the listener is saying, "Do you mean . . .?" so that the writer can say, "No, not quite. What I mean is . . ." or "Yes, but let me put it this way. . . ." Or even—and this is pay dirt— "Yes, I *was* saying that, but *now* I want to say. . . ." Sayback helped her move past her original thinking.

In short, sayback is an invitation to the writer to find *new* words and thoughts—to *move* in her thinking. Sayback helps the writing (and the writer) to continue to cook, bubble, percolate. Sayback helps the writer think about what she *hasn't yet said* or even thought of.

Thus, though sayback is useful any time, it is particularly useful at an early stage in your writing: before you have struggled, agonized, or tried to get it just right—when you have just written in an exploratory way and things haven't jelled yet, when you haven't finally decided what it all adds up to.*

Guidelines for Sayback Responding

To the writer:

- Read your piece twice. Allow a bit of silence after both readings: don't rush even though you might feel nervous. Give your listener some time to collect her impressions.

---

*We are grateful to have learned about the use of sayback responding from Sondra Perl and Elaine Avidon of the New York City Writing Project.

- Listen openly to the listener's sayback. Accept whatever invitations or questions she extends and see if what she says leads you to *different* words—or even different thoughts—and say them. If this happens, you might want to take a few notes.

- Don't feel stuck with what you've already written; don't defend it. Keep your mind open and receptive: think of this as help in *shifting, adjusting, refining your thinking.*

To the listener:

- Don't worry about whether you like or don't like something: that's irrelevant here. Listen and get engaged with what you hear.

- After listening, try to sum up in a sentence or two what you feel the writer is really *getting at.* Say it in a mildly questioning tone so the writer can respond—perhaps by simply agreeing and saying, "Yes," but perhaps by putting her thoughts in somewhat different words. Think of yourself as inviting the writer to *restate* and thereby get *closer* to what she is really wanting to say.

- If the writer adjusts or changes what she wants to say, you may be tempted to add, "Oh, then you ought to make the following changes in your piece." Don't. Don't give *any* suggestions or advice about the writing itself. Leave all that to the writer. (We'll soon get to methods for giving that sort of feedback.)

You can do this in pairs or with groups of two to four listeners. After each listener gives sayback, the writer responds.

ooooo

Sample of Sayback (IIA) for "An Orange Basketball Game"

We will illustrate each kind of response with sample feedback on two pieces of student writing ("An Orange Basketball Game" and "Cleaning Up the Environment," reprinted on pages 6–8).

One Reader

You are telling me how excited you get when you go to the game? You are trying to take me there? You are saying that everyone else gets excited about who wins, but for you the excitement is being there—winning doesn't matter? Is that it?

14

Another Reader

You want me to experience what it's like sharing support for a team? You want to focus in on the feelings of the fans and the physical environment rather than on the game itself?

How a Writer Might Think about This Feedback

It's not exactly excited I get. Somehow just caught up; absorbed. As far as bringing readers there, I don't really think about readers—I'm writing this for me—this draft anyway. And I want to get across the connection between the team and the fans too—what it's like when everyone—such a huge crowd—has certain emotions based on what ten players do. Maybe I better start thinking about readers now. I'm mixed up about the score business. Winning does matter, yet it doesn't matter too. I have to figure out what I really want to say.

Sample of Sayback (IIA) for "Cleaning Up the Environment"

One Reader

You are really angry—seething—about how people leave garbage around—especially your roommates? But you are trying to be controlled and rational, to take a larger view and give a sensible argument for how to deal with the problem?

Another Reader

Trashing the environment is a terrible problem but there is, in fact, a solution?

IIB. DESCRIPTIVE RESPONDING:
Pointing
Summarizing
What's Almost Said or Implied
Center of Gravity

This is a group of ways to give descriptive, noncritical feedback:

- *Pointing.* Which words, phrases, or features of the writing do you find most striking or memorable (or which do you like best)?

- *Summary.* What do you hear the piece saying? What's the main meaning or message?

15

- *What's Almost Said or Implied.* What do you think the writer is going to say but doesn't? What ideas seem to hover around the edges? What do you end up wanting to hear more about?

- *Center of Gravity.* What do you sense as the generative center or the source of energy? (The center of gravity might *not* be the main point. Sometimes an image, phrase, detail, or digression seems a point of special life or weight in the piece. The center of gravity might be something minor that is "trying" to be major.)

It helps if listeners think of themselves as allies or co-writers with the writer.

These questions can be used at any stage in a piece of writing. They're good at an early exploratory stage because the answers don't give you any criticism. Instead of readers standing off to one side and judging, these questions get them to jump in and help you with your thinking and writing. Readers give *you* ideas.

But they are good questions for later stages of writing too. Even after you have agonized over a piece of writing, you always need to know what *got through* to readers before you get any other feedback. You can't trust criticism or any other feedback unless you first know what the readers *think* you are saying. Sometimes too, you agonize over a piece yet still feel fragile about it and decide to hold off any criticism for a while. Criticism is not necessarily what improves your writing.

ooooo

Sample Descriptive Responses (IIB) for "An Orange Basketball Game"

One Reader

- *Pointing*
    — I like the energy of the writing. The sound of a voice right from the first sentence. "Of course, we're here an hour early."
    — "On which ten college men . . . round metal hood . . . &c." It's like a man from Mars describing basketball. It makes me see the familiar as strange.
    — "The high is much higher than the low is low." "Tip-off."
    — The long paragraph in the middle that picks out all the sounds within the loud roar. And those "cement benches."

- *Summary*
    — Sentence: Let me give you the excitement of going to a Syracuse University home basketball game at the Carrier Dome.
    — Word/image: The game, tumultous sea of orange.

16

- *Almost Said.* It doesn't matter who wins, really. It's a ridiculous game, but I love it. I need excitement in my life—to get out of myself. (Also, perhaps this): I am *so* upset that the team doesn't do better that I can't even bear to think about winning or losing. I've got to make fun of people who worry about who wins. This is why I can't bear to tell you about the second half of the game.

- *Center of Gravity.* The roar of sounds that contains all the other individual sounds inside it; or the odor of hot dogs, mustard, sweat, beer, and stale air-conditioned ventilation—and rising temperature.

Another Reader

- *Pointing.* All the orangeness and the words about the bandanas being free. The stuff about fans thinking the team hears each of them. Portable cushions for older fans. 32,000 eyes.

- *Summary*

  — Sentence: It's wonderful to be a part of a group of fans.

  — Word/image: clamor, orangeness.

- *Almost Said.* Fans may seem disappointed at a loss, but the true reason for going to a game is to be part of a cheering crowd—share common feelings with others. One can lose oneself, get outside of oneself—this is all right (I think) even if the whole affair is a bit trivial.

- *Center of Gravity.* Noise, made up of various components. Physicality: colors, smells, food.

How A Writer Might Think about This Feedback

I like the "sea of orange" summary. I'm still not pleased about "give you the excitement." Is that what my piece really sounds like or just one reader's translation? It sounds too corny. Is my piece corny?

Interesting thought that I'm really upset about the team losing. I do feel very sad about the team's record. All those trips to the stadium to see them lose. But I don't feel I'm really hiding anything. But that reader does make me wonder why I avoided talking about the second half of the game. Somehow it feels right to avoid it—or I *wanted* to write about the first half and stop before the game is done. I wonder why? I guess this is what I want to think about more in revising.

Am I trying to get outside myself; is this some personal escape tactic—or a society's escape? Is it too idea-less or do I want it that way? Something else to think about for revision. I don't really want to get philosophical—or at least I don't think I do.

17

I didn't think of those "centers of gravity" as central, but they were the parts I ended up liking most.

Sample Descriptive Responses (IIB) for "Cleaning Up the Environment"

One Reader

- *Pointing.* (After one reading): The section about your roommate and dishes in the bathroom. It's not worth cleaning up his mess because it won't make any difference. "A certain radius." "Make them eat it." "Legislatures." "My opponents argue." "Animals." (After second reading): Problems in the home. "In my suite, however, there is a problem." "I am asking for a little help." I like the grappling with a hard issue—the caring.

- *Summary*

  — Sentence: I need help doing something about all the garbage and litter in the world.

  — Word/image: Garbage.

- *Almost Said.* I hear two opposite unstated messages almost said: (1) "It's hopeless." (2) "We *can* do something about it." Not sure which I hear louder. Also, "I'm scared." I want to hear more about things that could be done—though I'm not sure whether that is central to where the essay is going.

- *Center of Gravity.* Dishes in the bathroom; garbage near the campsite.

IIC. DESCRIPTIVE RESPONDING:
Structure
Voice, Point of View, Attitude toward the Reader
Level of Abstraction or Concreteness
Language, Diction, Syntax

In literature classes we tend to *describe* what is going on in a story, poem, or novel, rather than to judge it or find mistakes. Inherent in such an approach is *respect for the text*: the result is learning—allowing the text to speak on its own. You can benefit from asking for that kind of respect for your writing and from showing that kind of respect to the writing of others—even if this writing is not yet famous and studied in literature classes.

But it's not easy to *describe* what is going on in a piece of writing or how the piece works. It helps to use categories to describe important dimensions of a piece of writing.

- *Structure.* How is the piece organized? Note that there's no such thing as "no organization." You can always describe what serves as the beginning, the middle parts, and the end.

- *Voice, Point of View, Attitude toward the Reader.* How would you describe the voice you hear (e.g., objective, tentative, whispering)? What is his point of view or position or stance on the subject: does he speak from an objective position or as an involved participant? (And does he speak in first, second, or third person?) How does he seem to treat the reader (condescending, pleading)?

- *Level of Abstraction or Concreteness.* How much generalization and how much detail or example?

- *Language, Diction, Syntax.* What kind of words are used (technical, down to earth, full of metaphors and images)? What kind of sentences and phrasing (simple, complex, lots of pauses and inversions)?

Because this kind of feedback requires *acts of analysis,* readers cannot give it after just hearing your piece, even twice. They need your text in their hands so they can go back over it. Readers *can* get by without a text if they listen and work together to produce collective answers. (By the way, using this kind of feedback gives good practice for literature classes.)

Make sure readers describe the text in as "descriptive" or nonevaluative terms as possible—not praising or criticizing. Thus if they start to say, "The paper is full of babyish sentences," point out the value judgment there and ask them to get rid of it, perhaps saying instead, "The paper is full of short sentences with simple syntax." Try to get them also to describe *where* these sentences occur and where the longer ones are.

ooooo

Sample Descriptive Responses (IIC) for "An Orange Basketball Game"

One Reader

- *Structure.* The piece is a story or narrative; it moves straight through time. But it doesn't "move"; rather it *stops* at different moments (one hour before; opening moment; last minutes of first half; half time). But the emphasis is on description in space and mood, not time.

- *Voice, Point of View, Attitude toward Reader.* Excited voice, yet a sense of her being alone in the middle of tumult. It's told in the first person: a person with her brother (though I forgot about the brother except at

19

PROCESS BOX

I spent a long time writing a good draft of a memo to teachers in the writing program. I was making suggestions for an evaluation process I wanted them to use. (I wanted them to write reflectively about their teaching and visit each other's classes.) I worked out a plan very carefully and at the end I really *wanted* them all to do this—realizing of course that some would not want to. The more I thought about it, the more I felt I was right. I ended up putting it very strongly: they *have* to do it.

I read my draft out loud in a staff meeting to Pat, Bruce, Jeff, Aaron, and Cindy. Wanted feedback. People were slow to bring up that final bit (that they *have* to do it), but finally Cindy brought it up bluntly as a problem. Some disagreed and said, in effect, "Yes, we've got to insist." But Bruce and Jeff thought the way I wrote it went too far— would get readers' backs up unnecessarily. ("I don't want to be inflammatory," I said, and Aaron replied, "But you seem to want to make a flame.")

I wanted to defend what I wrote, but I held back; but the impulse to defend kept recurring. Finally I saw that I *could* make my point more mildly—and it would get my point across *more* effectively. I could see it was better the milder way. Finally I ended up feeling, "That's what I *wanted* to say."

I tell the story—it came to me this morning as I woke up early— as a paradigm of how feedback can and should work: of writing as a potentially collaborative social process. That is, it now strikes me that I *needed* to write those things; I needed to punch it to them. But by having the chance to read it out loud to this surrogate audience rather than the real one—an audience with whom I felt safe—peers—I could as it were "get it said." And then listen; and finally hear.

By the end I felt comfortable and grateful at the outcome—even though of course some little part of me still experienced it as having to "back down" and "accept criticism." Yet by the end, it didn't feel like backing down and "doing it their way." By the end it was what *I* wanted to say.

In short, the process of reading a draft to a safe audience and getting feedback wasn't just a way to "fix" my draft. The main thing was that *it allowed my mind to change.* My intention ended up being different from what it had been.

PETER ELBOW, 3/84

the beginning and the end). The narrator identifies with the others ("they're just like me"), but she is kind of apart and in herself and standing back and describing them from the outside too. Is she talking to herself, not us? I certainly don't get a sense of her talking "up" to us or "down" to us. I guess we are overhearing her talking to herself.

- *Level of Abstraction or Concreteness.* It works more by way of concrete details: "hard floor," "ten college men," "one foot in diameter orange ball," "stocky pivot guard," "cold concrete benches." A lot of adjectives. Not much metaphor: "balloon-like roof," "orange sea," although this latter one is powerful. I don't feel much generalization or abstraction.

- *Language, Diction, Syntax.* Plain everyday conversational language; a sense of these words as *spoken*—yet not particularly informal, slangy, or even "conversational." Direct and *clear*. Some use of punchy phrasing: "These fans are tough." "high higher . . . low low." Energy injected by quite a lot of reported speech (or thought) by others: quotations.

Another Reader

- *Structure.* A story. Events in a time sequence cause changes in mood, but the emphasis is on mood changes. Begins and ends with focus on what's happening to the "I"—and much less of that in center parts—which makes a kind of neat "frame" for the story.

- *Voice, Point of View, Attitude toward Reader.* An "I-report" of a person very tuned into details of sound and sight. Here's the tone of voice I hear: "You may wonder why I think this is so exciting, but I'm going to try to just feel it and live through it. I sort of hope you'll indulge me in this and maybe let me get you caught up too because of my enthusiasm—even though you really aren't much of a sports fan."

- *Level of Abstraction or Concreteness.* Concrete: color, smells are particularly evident. What such activity looks like. Physical sense of crowd. Still emphasis is on emotions. I can't think of any specific generalizations, and yet I feel a sense of generalization in the whole thing. Maybe if I looked back more carefully I'd find more generalization than I'm able to remember. That wouldn't surprise me.

- *Language, Diction, Syntax.* Informal, conversational—relevant to subject. Use of direct quotations adds zip. Occasional slang: "blow out," "luck shot," but pretty much stays away from sports jargon. Staccato rhythm at times (see second paragraph in particular). Syntax feels like speech. Occasional exaggeration ("extreme anticipation"). Sense of an additive style, details being continuously added, even piled up, just as they might occur to an observer.

How a Writer Might Think about This Feedback

I'm definitely not writing for a sports enthusiast; there isn't enough about the game itself, and the language is not sportsy (actually I don't know that language well enough). And, yes, I suppose I do wonder how serious people might react—but I think it's okay. Am I being defensive I wonder? The orange really did look like a sea—all the waves and undulations when people started waving orange things. I'm afraid if I did more generalization, it would cut into the mood. I'm glad it's underplayed a bit—maybe I could even underplay it more.

I'm not sure about my slight sarcasm—whether it was really gone by the end. If so, I wonder why, or I wonder if I could show somehow how that happened. Seems as though the readers didn't get it.

I am a people person, so I'm glad that came through—though, frankly, I wasn't thinking about that at all! I'm not sure I exactly understand how one makes syntax like speech, although I'm glad it sounds that real. Still, can one do that and be at all philosophical? Because I keep thinking I'd like it to be a bit more reflective.

Sample Descriptive Responses (IIC) for "Cleaning Up the Environment"

One Reader

- *Structure.* A general plea. Then two main examples: canoeing and the dorm room. Then attending to people who disagree. Finally talking about ways to do something about it.

- *Voice, Point of View, Attitude toward Reader.* First person: lots of "I." A somewhat preachy voice—at times a whiney sound. He's very caught up in the issue, very partisan. The sound of strong feelings somewhat held in check—working at being rational and somewhat controlled. At times I feel a helpless note—as though deep down he doesn't believe there's any hope at all.

- *Level of Abstraction or Concreteness.* Very much both: a large general claim—talking about garbage and damage to the environment at the largest level, yet it's full of very concrete and specific examples.

- *Language, Diction, Syntax.* Informal, slightly colloquial language ("I think it is disgusting the way people don't"). As though it's overheard speech. But there's also some rather detached "essay language" ("receptacle," "of a certain radius," "Some of my opponents have argued that").

IID. DESCRIPTIVE RESPONDING: METAPHORICAL DESCRIPTIONS

It turns out that you can usually see a faint star better out of the corner of your eye than when you look at it directly. You notice the same thing when in the middle of the night you try to see the faint luminous dial of the bedside clock: a squint from the corner of your eye usually does better. So too, it turns out that we can often capture more of what we know about something if we talk *indirectly*—through metaphor—than if we try to say directly what we see. For metaphorical feedback, get readers to describe what you have written in the following terms:

- *Weather(s)*. What is the weather of the writing: sunny? drizzling? foggy? Try describing different weathers in different parts.

- *Clothing*. How has the writer "dressed" what he has to say? In faded denims? formal dinner wear? in a carefully chosen torn T-shirt?

- *Substitute Writing*. Pretend the writer wrote this instead of something very different that was on her mind. What was that something different?

- *Shape*. Picture the shape of the piece—perhaps even in a drawing.

- *Color(s)*. If the writing were a color, what would it be? Different colors at different spots?

- *Animal(s)*. Ditto.

- *Writer-to-Reader Relationship*. Imagine a picture that symbolizes the relationship of the writer to the reader.

In order to give metaphorical feedback, you must enter into the spirit of the enterprise: be a bit playful. Don't strain or struggle for answers: just say the answers that come to mind even if you don't understand them or know why they come to mind. Some of the answers may be "off the wall"— and some of the really good answers may *seem* off the wall at first. Just give answers. Trust the connections your mind comes up with.

The writer too must listen in the same spirit: just listening and accepting and not struggling to figure out what these answers *mean*. The writer, like the responder, needs to trust that there *is* useful material in there—even if it's mixed with things that aren't so useful. Eat like an owl: the owl swallows the mouse whole and trusts its organism to sort out what is useful and what's not. You too can listen in an attitude of trust, and *your* mind will use what makes sense and ignore what does not.

There's a side benefit to this kind of feedback. It highlights an important truth for almost all feedback: that we are not looking for "right answers," we're looking for individual perceptions—ways of seeing. And it all works best if there is a spirit of play and trust.

23

(Two kinds of feedback that you've already tried out are really meta-phorical: center of gravity and voice. We included them earlier because they fit so well in those earlier contexts; obviously they belong here too.)

ooooo

Sample Metaphorical Responding (IID) for "An Orange Basketball Game"

One Reader

- *Weather(s)*. It's clear and sunny, but through the middle the wind comes up and it gets blustery, but at the end, suddenly calm and windless.

- *Clothing*. It's a comfortable, well-worn jacket. It has a few wrinkles and stains, but it looks good and keeps you warm even in a chill.

- *Substitute Writing*. She's a little sad that she recently tried out for the swim team and didn't make it.

- *Shape.*

- *Color(s)*. I see the piece as blue, clean, and luminous.

- *Animal(s)*. I see it as a frisky goat.

- *Picture of Writer-to-Reader Relationship*. The writer is taking me by the hand and leading me carefully as though she is an older sister, explaining everything to me in a concerned way. But then she gets all involved in what she's saying and forgets all about me, forgets to hold my hand. But I stay with her and feel safe and close all the same (the opposite of feeling like a child who has lost his mommy in Macy's on a busy day).

- *Center of Gravity*. Roar of sounds.

- *Voice*. Hard to answer. I hear excitement, yet a quiet voice—almost no voice. Now that I look again, I see a perky and assured voice in that opening sentence ("of course we're here an hour early") and a motherly assured voice explaining to me about the dome. But then I feel it drifting off and not talking to me anymore but rather musing to herself. I want to call it a silent but excited voice inside her head.

A Second Reader

- *Weather(s).* Bright, sunshiny, blocked out at times by thin clouds. Winds blow hard on occasion and on occasion die down.

- *Clothing.* It's a lively, brightly colored sweat suit but with a rip in the left knee.

- *Substitute Writing.* She's thinking about how much she's going to miss her brother when he goes away; how sad she'll be.

- *Shape.*

- *Color(s).* Red-orange, patches of yellow, mixed up with pieces of brown.

- *Animal(s).* Bear rummaging in underbrush looking for something, shaking itself, and pawing the ground every so often.

- *Picture of Writer-to-Reader Relationship.* Writer is talking to me out of a crowd, but there's a little space around her—no spaces elsewhere. Or else maybe she's bouncing around on waves—sometimes the boat rocks violently, sometimes it rocks gently. But the voice mostly stays the same. I'm on shore close enough to hear but not troubled by tossing waves.

- *Center of Gravity.* Physicality: colors, smells, foods.

- *Voice.* It's the voice of a young person, pulling out of adolescence, beginning to get perspective on her own perceptions. Sarcastic at times ("I think they might be a little nervous"). But unable to resist crowd excitement. Although it is not particularly excited, it records excitement. Any excitement is because of subject, not the game itself. Voice is not that of a die-hard fan.

What a Writer Might Think about This Feedback

I'll just listen. But I guess I get a vague sense that readers think I'm ambiguous, being pulled in and resisting and then becoming part of crowd. I want the confusion to remain, but also some sense of calm.

I don't really think I'm confident about the ending of the game—by saying I'm confident I'm being a certain kind of fan, giving myself to the experience, not drawing back anymore. I'm not sure whether I'd sit quietly through the remainder of the game or roar and yell like all the others. Maybe I've accepted my part in this place. I could write an essay about fan psychology—but I don't want to. Or about the place of spectator sports in my life—but I don't want to—although I'd like that to come through.

I'm not sure why one reader sees this as blue and the other as red-orange. Seem like opposites, but maybe they are both true. Yet both readers fantasize that I'm sad. I guess I can see that: something sad lying under all this excitement and fun, though I don't really know what it's about. A frisky goat but one who settled down? A bear looking for something? Perhaps, but I think I find it, and if I was a bear, I'd go back to my den satisfied.

Sample Metaphorical Responding (IID) to "Cleaning Up the Environment"

- *Weather.* Stormy and very windy, but with little patches of no wind.

- *Clothing.* Old and worn but newly laundered clothes. A new pair of socks that somehow clash.

- *Substitute Writing.* He's wondering, slightly worrying, about whether he'll get to be really good friends with his roommate.

- *Shape.* Like a snake that has swallowed an elephant.

- *Color(s).* Patchy gray and blue.

- *Animal(s).* A mule that is angry but dogged.

- *Picture of Relationship to Reader.* He has come across some trash and has just run over to a friend's room in total exasperation to *sound off* in fury. But there is someone else there with the friend—someone the writer doesn't know. So he tries to temper his impulse to shout and pound the table; he tempers it with reasonable suggestions and *thinking* about the problem. But it is a struggle. The listeners are sitting with their mouths hanging open.

- *Center of Gravity.* Dishes in the bathroom, garbage in the campground.

- *Voice.* The voice breaks back and forth between being loudly furious and then swallowing and holding on to the table and talking quietly— trying reasonably to see what can be done.

26

III

Analytic Responding

A. Skeleton Feedback
B. Believing and Doubting
C. Descriptive Outline

IIIA. ANALYTIC RESPONDING: SKELETON FEEDBACK

A good way to analyze the reasoning in a persuasive or argumentative essay
(or in any essay that is trying to assert something or make a point) is to get
readers to answer the following questions:

1. Reasons and Support

- What is the main point/claim/assertion of the whole paper?

- What are the main reasons or subsidiary points? (It's okay to list them
  as they come—in any order.)

- Taking each reason in turn, answer these questions:

  — What support, backing, or argument is given for it?

  — What support *could* be given?

  — What counter arguments or attacks could be made against this
    reason?

2. Assumptions

- What assumptions does the paper seem to make? What does the paper seem to take for granted?

3. Readers or Audience

- Who is the implied audience? Who does the writer seem to be talking to?

- Looking at the reasons, arguments, and assumptions, tell what kind of readers would tend to accept which ones (and what kind of readers would reject them).

- How does the writer *treat* the audience? as enemies? friends? equals? children? What's the stance toward audience?

About Using Skeleton Feedback

It probably makes most sense for readers to answer these questions in writing and at leisure—with the text in hand. However, you *could* get this kind of feedback orally if you have a group and the members cooperate in working out shared answers for each question.

The power in skeleton feedback comes from the *distance* and *detachment* it gives you from your piece of writing. Thus, it is particularly useful when you feel all tangled or caught up in your piece from having worked long and closely on it. (By the way, all three procedures for analytic responding have a kind of power that makes them particularly useful ways for you to *give yourself feedback* on an essay of your own. The questions provide you with a perspective that you otherwise lack on your own writing.)

Skeleton feedback is useful not only on later drafts when you are trying to test out the strength of your revised reasoning, but also on early drafts when you want help in figuring out what you really want to say—and how to organize it or what to emphasize. Skeleton feedback is a kind of cooperative mode where readers add to and sharpen your thinking for you.

A word about finding or uncovering assumptions. We make assumptions all the time: we can't talk without making assumptions. We *notice* assumptions all the time too, but sometimes it's hard to notice our noticing—or hard to find words for what we notice. Some assumptions are more obvious than others. By way of illustration, here are some assumptions that are implicit in our writing of this book:

- that writing is a struggle for most people.

- that writers of a textbook tend to be seen as, in one way, more than usually trustworthy (as authorities who are sticking to what is known and not trying to put anything over on readers). But in another way textbook writers are very *little* trusted because they don't seem human.

- that most of our readers want to work on writing—deep down—but that some of them will resent being made to do so.

- that we will be more persuasive if we are open about our prejudices.

Obviously some of these assumptions are questionable.

Arguments, in particular, always involve assumptions. Here, for example, are some common assumptions that turn up unstated in many arguments—assumptions that actually need to be questioned: that experts are usually righter than amateurs; that the majority should always rule; that what is modern is better than what is old. Here are two specific suggestions for uncovering assumptions:

- Look above at your answer to the question, "What support *could* be given?" for each reason or claim. Your answer might well constitute an assumption: an idea or argument or piece of evidence that the argument assumed was true.

- Look also at your answer to the question, "What attacks or counter arguments could be made?" on each reason or claim. Here too your answer might illustrate an assumption (e.g., "Your argument for recycling garbage assumes that people will take the trouble to separate their paper and their bottles from the rest of their trash; but that is unlikely").

○○○○○

Sample Skeleton Feedback (IIIA) on "Cleaning Up the Environment"*

First Reader

Main claim. The problem of fouling the environment is serious and we have to do something about it.

Reasons and support

- People don't care. (Support: evidence of people throwing things down, trash all around on the ground, the garbage at the riverside campground.)

- If people would only care and take a little time, things would be much better. (Support: Not much; it's mostly just an assertion.)

---

*Skeleton feedback doesn't fit the first paper about the basketball game since it's not trying to argue or assert anything.

29

- If people who made messes realized how much others were bothered by the messes, they wouldn't do it. (Support: Not much. Writer implies that he knows roommate well enough to know it's true of him.)

- *I* am disgusted and furious. (Support: tone of language, vividness of examples.)

- We can clean things up with everyone chipping in time and money—and legislation. (Support: None; just asserted as common sense.)

- Animals are hurt. (Support: None; just asserted as common sense.)

Assumptions

- People can be mobilized.

- The world can be made better.

- Telling how awful things are (and how bad I feel) will make a difference—change people's minds and behavior.

- People can work things out if they communicate their needs and feelings.

- *Recognizing* the objections of others—acknowledging them—will help defuse them, even if one doesn't offer an answer to them.

Readers and audience

- He seems to be talking to neutral bystanders. He's not treating us like the enemy. However, he is so angry and, at times, scolding, that some of it spills over and makes me feel a bit uncomfortable. I guess he's half sounding off his frustration to us, half trying to persuade us. Not sure. Is he perhaps implying that these (we) neutral bystanders are also petty offenders (chewing-gum–wrapper throwers) who might be persuaded to mend their ways?

- I guess the scolding seems *directed* at the offenders even though he doesn't quite *talk* to them. The arguments that reasonable and well-meaning people should pitch in and do something are most appropriate for us neutral bystanders.

Second Reader

Main claim. People should not litter.

Reasons and support

- It's disgusting to look at.

  — campground

— dorm room
— people don't want to use dirty places.

- It's unfair to those who try to keep things clean.

  — dorm room
  — will discourage others from cleaning up but encourage them to become litterbugs also.

- Will the results outweigh costs of cleaning up?
  — People in clean neighborhoods don't know how bad it is.
  — It's a waste because it will just get littered again.
  — Fewer people will get sick and that would save money.
  — When people become more used to cleanliness, they won't litter so much.

- What people can do to help:
  — raise money
  — donate money
  — Everyone can help a little.
  — Laws against littering could be harsher.
  — Neighborhoods can organize clean-up squads.

- Would benefit animal life
  — Animals can't clean up for themselves.
  — may make some species extinct or drive them away

Assumptions

- that other people find trash disgusting too

- that other people feel some obligation to the environment and to other people

- that people can be shamed into being cleaner

- that people in high-priced neighborhoods don't litter

- that litterbugs expect others to clean up after them

- that someone who makes a mess in a dorm room litters outside also

- that animals are important to the quality of human life

Readers or audience. People most likely to accept the argument: those who don't litter; those who care about the environment and plant and animal life; those who like natural beauty and who like to go camping, hiking, etc.; perhaps those opposed to pollution from chemicals, nuclear waste, and so on.

People most likely to object to the argument: those who want to decrease government spending; those who don't care much for the out-of-doors; those who litter (?); those who believe that everyone is responsible only for himself.

IIIB. ANALYTIC RESPONDING: BELIEVING AND DOUBTING

Here is a kind of response that zeroes in on the *content* or *ideas* in your writing. It invariably gives you more ideas, more material. The obvious place to use it is with essays, but if you ask readers to play the believing and doubting game with your stories, you'll get interesting feedback too.

Believing. Simply ask readers to *believe* everything you have written—and then tell you what that makes them notice. Even if they disagree strongly with what you have written, their job is to *pretend* to agree. In this way they will act as your ally: they can give you *more* reasons or evidence for what you have written; they can think of different and better ways of saying or thinking about what you have written.

Doubting. Now ask readers to pretend that everything is false, to find as many reasons as they can why you are wrong in what you say (or why your story doesn't make sense).

About using believing and doubting. Believing is harder for most people than doubting. Here are things that help:

- Remember it is a game. Just pretend.
- Role play. Instead of being yourself, pretend to be someone else who *does* believe the piece—and think of the things this person would see and say.
- Imagine a different world where everything that the piece says is true: enter into that fictional world and tell what you see. Or tell the story of what a world would be like where everything that the piece says is true.

Usually it makes sense to start with the believing game. First, find all the possibilities and richness in what you have written: build it up before tearing it down. But if readers have trouble believing—if they are inveterate doubters and can't turn off that habit—they sometimes benefit from playing the doubting game first. This can get the doubting out of their system or satisfy that skeptical itch, and afterward they sometimes find themselves freer to *enter into* a way of thinking that is foreign to them.

See my journal entry of this date on this disk. About how I react to feedback from ———— and ———— on my "Believing" essay. They give me critical feedback. ———— in particular is quite fierce about how I made him into the enemy; I made him mad.

The feedback from both of them is enormously useful, but it makes me uncomfortable and mad. I'm all stirred up. It leaves me upset and unable to sleep or relax. I think the crucial factor is that it doesn't feel like it's coming from an ally. I feel I have to fight. That's the main response: wanting to fight them. Energized for fight. Aggression. Unable to relax. Unable to put it aside. Caught.

I guess you could call that useful. It certainly triggers a piece of my character that is strong. I'm a fighter. My intellectual life is, in a way, a fight. (Perhaps I should talk about this in the Believing essay. I'm in combat.) But it's so exhausting always to be in combat. Yes, it is energizing; it keeps one going. But is it really the best way to go? I wonder if it brings out the *best* thinking. Thinking with my dukes up too much?

Compare the effect of this feedback with the effect of the feedback I got from Paul on the same draft. It was so energizing and comforting. But not sleepy comforting. It made me go back to my thoughts and ideas. It got me *unstuck* from the adversarial defensive mode where I'm trying to beat these guys. It sent me back into my thoughts and simply had me explore what I had to say.

The comparison casts an interesting light on the public and private dimensions of writing. Feedback from ———— and ———— keeps me fixated on *them*—on audience. I want to beat them. Paul's feedback sends me back into myself and helps me forget about audience.

What I'm curious about is whether this present upset, stirred up reaction is *unproductive* fighting. Arid and unfruitful? I wish I could forget all about it, put aside all memory of their criticism and just write what I want to write. Just explore my own train of thought.

But I probably have to admit that the turmoil does help; it keeps the pot bubbling. Though I don't like my condition. I'm mad, and I can't sleep or relax, and I feel like it's eating me up. There's clearly a compulsive element to it; it's getting in the way of my just plain living in present time reality and with other people and relaxing. Nevertheless, *because I have confidence that there's something good in what I'm writing* (partly thanks to Paul), I'm not going to give up. I'm going to go on and make it good. But if I were younger and less secure (!) in what I was doing, it would discourage me more or hold me back.

PETER ELBOW, 10/84

You don't necessarily need to get *both* kinds of feedback. In fact, if you are working on an early draft—or if you feel very fragile about something you have written—it can be very useful to get *only* the *believing* responses. This is a way to ask people frankly to support and help you in making your case or imagining the world you are trying to describe. Conversely if you have a late draft that you feel confident about and are trying to prepare for a tough audience, you might ask only for doubting.

Readers need to learn a spirit of play to give this kind of response, and you, as writer, must also learn to take it all in a spirit of play. Especially the doubting. People can get carried away with the skeptical, wet-blanket game. (School trains us in trying to doubt—not in trying to believe.) You will hear lots of reasons why what you wrote is *wrong*. Remember it is all a game, purposely exaggerated. Taken as a game, the doubting needn't bother you. What's more, this play dimension helps you take *all* feedback in the right spirit. For all feedback is really a process of looking at what you have written through various distorting lenses—to help you see what you can't see. After all this bending and distorting, you get to make up your own mind and make changes or not as you see fit.

ooooo

Sample Believing and Doubting (IIIB) Responses to "Cleaning Up the Environment"*

One Reader

Believing. It's a serious and important problem. We see the same issue on all fronts: in a small indoors living quarters, on the city streets, in the open space of the country, and on a global level.

People don't realize how much others care; and how much damage trash does to the environment. When they do, they realize it's in their own interest to take more care.

The small scale and the large scale can reinforce each other. On the small scale, people living together can communicate how much they care about the quality of their space—to affect the consciousness of the uncaring person. But they also need to end up with some rules to make it work. These rules need to grow out of discussion and be agreed on by all—thus a form of "legislation." Now this is the same process needed on the larger political scale: certain people communicating their need and their caring to other people; and pushing for and enforcing results through legislation.

But the key and the starting point has to be communication of *strong feeling* about how much harm comes from trashing the environment.

---

*We put the essay before the story, since essays are the more obvious arena for believing and doubting.

Doubting. There's no way to make people care. The society and culture have indoctrinated everyone into a throw-away mentality of not caring about other people. Scolding and venting self-righteous anger certainly won't do any good. There's no "legislating" that kind of caring—or doing it through bandwagon preaching or cheerleading.

In fact, there *is* no problem: we probably live in one of the cleanest environments ever: think about the London of Dickens's time with the lethal soot and fog.

Another Reader

Believing. You're certainly right—more people litter than don't litter—even people dressed nicely. They're so careful about their own appearance and don't seem to have a hair out of place, and yet they'll throw stuff on the ground. And storekeepers don't really keep their sidewalks very nice either. People are really lazy. I'd often like to walk up and ask people who they think is going to pick up their stuff—do they think that just because they pay taxes which pay the salaries of sanitation men—that they don't have to do anything? And it isn't only campgrounds; it's also public parks and beaches.

I bet students wouldn't treat their houses the way they treat their dorm rooms. It's just like they can't accept the responsibility that comes with being on their own. You people in this room are wimpy—you ought to pick up all his junk one day and just throw it on his bed—or else build a fence around his bed and just keep throwing things on the other side of it. This jerk needs a good lesson and you guys just seem to "take it." You ought to do it yourself if the others won't join you. What about bugs—or doesn't this guy leave food around? You'll take the bugs home and your mother will love it.

The animals that profit from litter are the rats, and they're dirty and spread diseases. You ought to make copies of this and just go around distributing it to people—because I bet that most of the people who litter really don't like the mess—they need to be reminded that they're causing it.

There's so much emotion in the essay, and people need to feel that emotion. And also the way you look at the larger picture and the personal picture at the same time makes me see that the two are related—if each of us did our share everywhere in dorm rooms and outside in the streets and parks, the environment would be better.

It's good that you brought up the bit about money because some people may not care about the environment who would care about having to put out tax money.

I like your mention of the possibility of laws at the end—makes me see that there are other strategies—and yet you don't get caught up in what the legislation should be.

35

Doubting. Where are you supposed to throw litter? There's never any receptacles when you need them—or else they are full. It's not really a matter of people who are "disgusting" or bad—it's a systemic problem. Some people just like to blame *people*—it makes them feel good: instead of looking for real causes. We live in a system that makes people have to want things and then throw them away; that makes companies make a profit by selling people things they don't need—and by packaging things in wrappings that are not necessary but make them look more glittery. It's the people who live in lovely well-kept homes and neighborhoods who complain—who turn up their noses at the dirtiness in poor neighborhoods—but they are really living off those poor people. It sounds to me like you are trying to run away from the complicated situation—from your guilt even—by shaking a scolding finger at others.

Sample Believing and Doubting Responses (IIIB) to "An Orange Basketball Game"

One Reader

Believing. When I try to enter in, I feel as though I'm already there. I look around more. I look up at the high ceiling and imagine the fretwork of beams; my mind goes up there and I imagine looking down on all this activity.

Then I look over at my brother's face during the game and take a special pleasure in how it is flushed with excitement—he's totally oblivious to me observing him—completely wrapped up in the excitement.

I'm excited and enjoying this game too, but I also enjoy a certain quietness inside me as part of my mind steps outside the scene and drinks in with a certain calmness.

Doubting. I'm jerked from moment to moment. I don't know what happens in between—especially don't know how the game ends. I don't believe there is a brother there.

Why mention him if you don't do anything with him? (But immediately my believing side jumps in: I kind of like the companionship—even the mystery.)

I don't believe that shot in the last ten seconds. Too corny. The writer made it up.

Couldn't have a basketball player named Pearl Washington. And all those people couldn't really get so excited.

I can't quite feel the quality of the half time: is it quiet or noisy? What's the feeling?

Another Reader

Believing. As a big fan of basketball, I can really get into what you're writing about. Part of the excitement is the fans—it's wonderful to have emotional reactions which are almost exactly the same as those of everyone else around you. Makes you forget other things and just live for the excitement of the moment. I hate it though when I have to watch a game on a big screen. It doesn't seem as real as the whole thing—still it's better than watching on TV because you still have the other fans around you. Basketball isn't an easy game—it's so fast paced and you have to think so quickly on your feet. Yeah, all the winning games easily make up for the losing games—although sometimes when there isn't a winning game for a long while, it's hard to keep up the spirit, and the crowds get smaller too.

When you're sitting waiting for the game to start, it seems like forever— the tension builds and builds and then it gets so quiet right when the game starts—and that's the most tension of all. The roaring crowds are such fun, but I'd like to know more about what's going on in the game—great shots? fouls? fights? I guess if you really think about the smells especially when it's hot, it could be a bit disgusting, but I don't really think I notice it very often.

The end of the half is always exciting, but I also find myself looking forward to some relief from the tension of the game—some chance to talk over what happened. It's hard to do that during the game—although you can shout things.

Doubting. No real basketball fan would pay so little attention to the game itself—you must not really know anything about the game—one of those people who just comes to be seen—to be able to say you were there. How could a real basketball fan be satisfied with just watching the game on some big screen? The whole thing is overdone—I don't think you're as excited as you try to make me think you are. And that silly business about describing the game just doesn't work. Or is that your real opinion—that it's a stupid game? You don't care about the game at all. And believe me, the lows are really low—that is, if you're really a fan. Building up the tension is really fake. What difference does it make if there's so much orange around. I don't think any of these people are true fans.

Those reported comments sound fake also—believe me, fans use much stronger language than that. You're so wrapped up in the noise you don't know what's happening on the court.

And why don't you tell me who wins? That proves it! You're not a fan, and I don't believe you know enough about the team to know whether they can win or not.

IIIC. ANALYTIC RESPONDING: DESCRIPTIVE OUTLINE

Where the skeleton feedback is useful on early exploratory writing as well as on late drafts, the descriptive outline doesn't make much sense unless the writing has been carefully shaped and revised. The descriptive outline involves an analysis of each paragraph—which isn't worth the effort unless the paragraphs have been worked over.

The descriptive outline (developed by Kenneth Bruffee) is more disciplined and analytic than skeleton feedback—but correspondingly more powerful. It involves a careful mini-analysis of the *meaning* and *function* of each paragraph. You can't really do a descriptive outline unless you have the text in hand and take time; and it makes most sense to write out the results. Because the structure of the descriptive outline gives such perspective on a text, it is a particularly useful form of feedback to give to *yourself*: it helps you see what you couldn't see before. Here are the steps.

For the whole piece:

- Write a "says" sentence: a one-sentence summary of what the whole piece is *saying*—its main point.

- Write a "does" sentence: a one-sentence summary of what the whole piece is *doing* or trying to do or accomplish with readers.

Do the same for each paragraph or section:

- Write a "says" or summary sentence.

- Write a "does" sentence that tells how that paragraph or section is *functioning* in the strategy of the whole essay, or what it is trying to do to readers.

It's not so easy to write these sentences—especially "does" sentences which explain the *function* a paragraph is performing. Here is an example of a "does" sentence:

This paragraph introduces an objection that some readers might feel, and then tries to answer that objection.

Avoid letting your "does" sentence just summarize or repeat your "says" sentence. The key is to *keep out of your "does" sentence any mention of the content of the paragraph.* You shouldn't be able to tell from a "does" sentence whether the essay is about cars or ice cream.

Here is an ineffective "does" sentence—it's really just a disguised "says" sentence:

This paragraph states the idea that women's liberation has affected men more than it has women.

To fix it, remove any mention of any of the *ideas* in the paragraph—and talk only about form or function:

This paragraph introduces the main point of the essay in a way that tries to surprise the reader or violate his expectations.

○○○○○

Sample Descriptive Outline (IIIC) of "An Orange Basketball Game"

One Reader

- Says, whole essay. The excitement of seeing a Syracuse University home basketball game is completely captivating.

- Does, whole essay. To *give* or make the reader *feel* the experience that is being described.

- Says, first paragraph. We come an hour early and look around to see the field house divided into two parts and the fans milling around, and we think about the game that is going to be played.

- Does, first paragraph. Sets the physical scene and tries to catch the reader up into the mood.

- Says, second paragraph. Ten minutes till it starts and I look around to see fans and players in place—waiting for the game to start.

- Does, second paragraph. Heightens the excitement; starts out appealing to the reader's time sense—zeroing in on a specific moment and only ten minutes to go. But the paragraph concentrates mostly on vision: sights and eyes.

- Says, third paragraph. The game starts, the first goal, Syracuse gets it, and the noise roars.

- Does, third paragraph. Zeroes in on an even smaller unit of time, yet concentrates on sound.

- Says, fourth paragraph. Pearl Washington of Syracuse gets the last score of the half with only ten seconds to go—breaking a tie.

- Does, fourth paragraph. Moves us forward to another exciting moment and, like preceding ones, tries to give us the experience—this time with smells and also an exciting happening (tie-breaking goal).

- Says, fifth paragraph. Everyone in the field house waits through the half—wondering "will they win?"

- Does, fifth paragraph. Moves the narrative forward in time, but emphasizes a quieter mood—relief from or contrast to the mood of the preceding two paragraphs.

- Says, last paragraph. We sit waiting and I am confident we'll win.

- Does, last paragraph. Zooms inside the head of the speaker—making things internal and quiet instead of external and noisy. Works for sense of ending by this contrast—and because it's so short: a kind of punch.

Another Reader

- Says, whole essay. Fan involvement in a basketball game is more exciting than the game.

- Does, whole essay. Makes me, as reader, feel the excitement and also feel that there's nothing wrong about being excited about something which, from some points of view, might seem silly.

- Says, first paragraph. Arrival at Carrier Dome, description of scene, brief talk of game—tiny bit tongue-in-cheek—characterizes hopes of fans.

- Does, first paragraph. Sets scene, introduces main theme, sets tone, including original awareness of writer toward major theme.

- Says, second paragraph. Almost game time, anticipation grows, focus on court itself.

- Does, second paragraph. Builds suspense, narrows focus of emotion and action.

- Says, third paragraph. Start of game and what happens just at beginning and then focuses back on fans.

- Does, third paragraph. Heightens suspense momentarily—returns to main theme.

- Says, fourth paragraph. Back to game, end of first half and what happens (Syracuse breaking tie). Combined focus on game and fans.

- Does, fourth paragraph. Builds suspense to climax, creates tension. Draws reader into physical setting.

- Says, fifth paragraph. What happens at half time, some description of age range of fans, concludes with fans' hopes for second half.

- Does, fifth paragraph. Creates a lull—slight restoration of tension at end, but not as intense.

- Says, sixth paragraph. How writer feels.

- Does, sixth paragraph. Reinforces my sense of main theme of piece. Shows that writer has accepted her attitude toward game.

How a Writer Might Think about This Feedback

I'm amazed to see how much "orderliness" that descriptive outline shows. Is my paper really that orderly, or does it come from this kind of summarizing?

Yes, I need to make more than one paragraph where I have the first one. But on the other hand, I don't want some neat "essay-like" scheme where each paragraph seems mechanically to have a topic. I want this to have a certain casual jumbled quality—after all, the whole point is that all these different impressions crowded in on me, and I want them to crowd in on the reader. I'm not trying to write an analysis.

I do think that's what I want—to make what happens on the court important only because it has certain effect on fans—although I still wonder if I shouldn't connect players and fans more. And I suppose I too feel somewhat as though it's a little silly to be so excited over something so insignificant. And yet the feeling of the fans—the unity of the crowd—feeling part of it: I hope the bit at the end—and not actually describing the end of the game—gives that feeling. Maybe I need to work on the beginning a bit—and maybe concentrate on age-range stuff earlier as it shows that we're not all crazy adolescents—but then maybe I'm feeling a sense of belonging to that wide range more at end than at beginning.

My brother being there was important—and I see that. Should it be more obvious? Or is it good to have subtlety of this person close to me and my simultaneous connection to sort of a faceless humanity? Both things are there.

Descriptive outline makes my final paragraph sound better than it is: but helps me see it new. I wasn't satisfied in writing it, still am not. It's because I still haven't figured out what I'm trying to do in the whole piece. I mean I like most things in it, but this feedback is helping me realize that I'm still stuck as to the "so what" or the why of it all.

Sample Descriptive Outline (IIIC) of "Cleaning Up the Environment"

One Reader

- Says, whole essay. The problem of litter and garbage is serious and needs to be addressed.
- Does, whole essay. Attempts to make readers feel how bad a problem is—to make them want to do something about it.
- Says, first paragraph. People have to start caring about the environment and doing something about trash.
- Does, first paragraph. States the main point right off; injects feeling.

41

- Says, second paragraph. It's bad everywhere: out in nature on a river-side campsite and at home in my dorm room.

- Does, second paragraph. Tries to give bite and vividness to the general plea by giving full and particular descriptions of two examples. Uses some story telling in the examples—to involve readers.

- Says, third paragraph. Some people say it's impossible or not worth trying to clean up environment, but I disagree.

- Does, third paragraph. Summarizes arguments by people who disagree with him.

- Says, fourth paragraph. Those who care can raise or donate money to help the problem.

- Does, fourth paragraph. Talks about a solution to the problem raised by the essay.

- Says, fifth paragraph. Trash hurts animals, and the whole problem needs to be dealt with by legislatures and individuals involved.

- Does, fifth paragraph. Brings in a new dimension of the problem. Suggests an approach for solving the whole problem—a different approach from the one suggested in the fourth paragraph.

IV

Reader-Based Responding: Movies of the Reader's Mind

The story of what goes on in readers is what we need most as writers: not evaluation of the quality of our writing or advice about how to fix it, but an accurate account of what our words did to readers. We need to learn to *feel* those readers on the other end of our line. When are they with us? When are their minds wandering? What are they thinking and feeling? What do they hear us saying?

Feedback would be simpler if it were just evaluation and advice: readers telling us which parts of our writing are weak and then telling us how to fix them. But there are a number of problems with this simple, practical approach:

- You can't *trust* people when they tell you what's weak and how to fix it. Even experts on writing usually *disagree* with each other. And when they agree about what's wrong, they usually disagree about how to fix it. (Notice how different it would be if we were doing arithmetic. Someone who knows arithmetic could point out every mistake and tell us how to fix it; and virtually all observers would agree.)

- Even if you *could* trust the judgment and advice of experts or writing teachers, it's hard to get much of their time. Even your own writing teacher has lots of students and not enough time to give really full feed-

43

back to everything you write. (Think about teachers reading and responding to *twenty-five or seventy-five papers at a time!*)

- And even if you had unlimited access to trustworthy experts and followed their advice and made all your writing terrific, you wouldn't *learn* as much as you should. You'd just be following their orders, not thinking for yourself.

Thus the importance of reader-based movies of the reader's mind: *get readers simply to tell you what happens inside their heads as they read your writing.* But this kind of feedback can be confusing (till you are used to it) because it gives you only the *facts* about writing—what went on in readers' minds—and the facts about writing are confusing. The same piece of writing causes different things to happen in different minds, and there's no direct advice in all this feedback about how to *fix* your writing.

So if you want *simple* feedback, you will have to settle for untrustworthy feedback. One person can tell you your problems and how to fix them, but the next person will tell you a different story. If you want *trustworthy* feedback, you have to settle for a mess. But it will be an interesting and useful mess. For you will gradually develop a sense for how readers react to your writing.

Movies of the reader's mind do not require experts. In fact sometimes you get wonderfully clear and helpful movies from children or very naive readers. But it does require honesty and trust. And it can be hard for some readers to learn to notice and describe their own reactions.

Thus many readers need help in learning to give you movies of their minds. Here are some ways to help them.

- *Serialize or Interrupt Your Text.* Read to them (or give them) your text one part at a time. At each interruption get them to tell you what's going on in their heads right at that moment. These "stop-frame movies" are particularly important near the beginning of your piece—after about a paragraph—so you can find out how your opening affects readers. In particular you need to know whether your opening has made them fight you or cooperate with you. Their reactions to the rest of your piece will depend on whether—early in their reading—they became sympathetic or resistant readers. Ask them if they are pedaling with you or dragging their heels as they read. If you give them a written copy of your piece—so they can see it better and take more time at home—persuade them to interrupt their reading at least two or three times and take notes of what's actually happening in their minds at the time of each interruption.

- *Get It in Story Form.* Get readers to tell their responses in the form of a story, e.g., "First I felt this, then I thought that," and so on. This prevents them from falling into useless global generalities like "I was interested" or "I liked it" or "It was exciting."

- *Get "I Statements."* If a reader says, "The third paragraph was boring," he hasn't given you an "I statement," but at least you can guess what was happening: *he* was bored in the third paragraph. Other readers might well *not* be bored. But if a reader says, "You should change this word or move that paragraph," you don't know what was happening to him. Was he bored, confused, or in disagreement? Get readers to tell their reactions in sentences starting with "I."

Movies of the reader's mind are probably the most useful all-around feedback. Indeed they involve all other forms of feedback since *anything* may go on in a reader's mind. But because they may well involve *judgment* or *criticism* we have held them till now—till you've tried other kinds of feedback and, we hope, developed trust in yourself and a relationship of trust and support with your readers. If readers are going to tell the truth about what your words did, you are liable to hear something like, "I was getting madder and madder because I felt this piece was so disorganized and misinformed, yet I also felt you were being condescending." It's hard to benefit from responses like that unless you feel them coming from a friend or ally.

When you get criticism, it helps to remember that the reader who is giving movies is not trying to criticize and not trying to reach a fair, impartial judgment (as in criterion-based feedback—which comes next). He is just trying to tell accurately what was occurring in him. It's clear that these are *his* subjective reactions and they might be unfair or wrong. He is not pretending to be God making an objective judgment.

Suggestions to the writer:

- This feedback requires honesty from readers. If you aren't getting honesty, perhaps it's *your* fault: you may not have convinced your readers that you really want honesty.

- If you want to get "unpolluted data" about what your words do, don't make apologies or introductions or explanations before they respond. (If it's an early draft, however, you may want to say a few words about what you were trying to do in your piece.)

- Don't quarrel with what a reader says—even if he utterly misunderstands what you wrote. You need to *learn about* readers' misreadings and mistakes—so you can think about whether your text needs changing. You're not trying to educate *readers* about your text, you're trying to get them to educate *you* about your text.

- *Invite exaggeration or parody.* This can be scary—but a big help if your readers are having trouble telling you what's happening to them or if they seem to be beating around the bush. For example, readers may feel vaguely bothered by something in your writing but be unable to

PROCESS BOX

Note: Our normal method of collaborating was for one of us to start a unit—do a very rough draft—and give it to the other to work on. The second person would just take it over—make it his or hers—make extensive changes—especially because the first version was often still quite unformed. Then what that second person produced would go back to the first person for more revision. All this usually on disks rather than on paper.

In this way we often lost track of who started something and who "owned" a section or an idea. We pretty much drifted or fell into this method: we were in a hurry, we knew we had a lot to write, and we didn't have time or energy to "protect" everything we wrote. Most of all we trusted each other. It worked remarkably well.

But for this particular unit we proceeded differently. Peter had worked out a fairly full outline and I took on the job of writing a draft from that outline. Then, instead of Peter taking it over from there—as we normally did—he wrote marginal feedback and gave it back to me to revise. (Peter was working on a couple of other units.) Thus we drifted into a problematic arrangement for this unit: I was writing a unit which felt like "Peter's"—and getting feedback from him about how to revise what I'd written.

I'm revising according to feedback and angry. Why doesn't he write the damn thing himself if he knows so surely what he wants. It's insulting—giving it back to me to do *his* way. I can't do it. I feel as though I'm not into it, not into the ideas—just into superficial stuff, trying to make it what someone else wants it to be. I'd like to just give it back to him and say that: "Here, you have such a sure idea about what this should be, why give it to me to do? I'm not a typist." Does he think I'm inept? stupid? Maybe he's right. Maybe I'm no good at this and he's saying these things so he won't have to say that. He doesn't think

explain what they feel—indeed scarcely even noticing that they feel anything. "It's ok," they'll say—"I pretty much liked what you wrote." If you feel brave enough to invite them to *exaggerate* their reaction, they will often find words for what's going on and say something like this: "If I exaggerated, I'd say you are beating me over the head here." You need to feel fairly secure before you ask for exaggeration because it may lead to a strong statement. But an element of play or humor can keep things from getting too sticky. For example, another helpful question is this: "What would a *parody* of my paper look like?" This ques-

"Life is unfair" is good. But I like it and I'll keep it. He wants this to be mainly a paper handed in to a professor in some other class, not an explanation for the self of something difficult. But I prefer the latter. So I kept trying to make the unit into what he wanted, while still thinking my idea was good.

But somehow (because he's a nice guy I guess) I kept on working with the suggestions. And as I wrote, I got caught up in thinking about getting students to see something two different ways: for themselves and for others. An interesting problem presented itself to me for solution. Could I make it work out that way? I began to explore, and suddenly it was *my* idea; although it wasn't suddenly—just my realization of what had happened seemed sudden. Apparently I was writing according to the feedback, and the idea became mine. I saw an interesting way to develop it, potential for the unit I hadn't seen before, ideas I had never written before. I got excited about it because it was good. Then I could write again without anger or resistance.

The feedback was gone; I really didn't look at any more of the marginal comments because they no longer mattered. I had my own way to go. I just forgot the way it had been done. When I finished up and polished it a bit, I looked back and who'd believe it! I had—on my own—come to saying almost exactly the same thing he said later on in the part of the feedback I hadn't even read. That's eerie! This must be an instance of authentically situated voice—somehow using the words and ideas of others and forging them in the furnace of my own word hoard. The ideas I got caught up with seemed to begin to write themselves out. But they also produced an interesting intellectual challenge to me. And there was something very satisfying about discovering that the two of us had been on the same wavelength—or close anyhow. His good ideas had fertilized my good ideas, and we ended up with something that was undoubtedly better than anything either of us could have done alone. It has been worth working through the anger.

PAT BELANOFF

tion also helps readers who can't explain what is going on in their heads as they read.

Suggestions to readers:

- Instead of trying to be judicious, your job is to show openly what's happening in you. This kind of feedback reveals just as much about *you* as it does about the writer. (Often the writer feels as though he is the only one revealing himself.)

- Don't quarrel with other readers. The more different the reactions, the more helpful they are for the writer. Quarreling about reactions is a waste of time—and will tend to make other readers scared to be honest, for fear someone will quarrel with them.

ooooo

Sample Movies of the Reader's Mind (IV) for "An Orange Basketball Game"

One Reader

I was sucked in immediately by the opening sentence with its spoken voice; as though I'm dropping into the middle of a conversation—but comfortable. Later on (rereading) I ended up troubled by how long the first paragraph was—how much diverse material was in it; messy. But the truth is that when I first read it I just steamed on through, happy as a clam. Nothing bothered me. Feeling the welter of impressions; sense of business.

I did pause and feel a moment's hesitation or uncertainty, however, at what I've been calling a Martian's view of basketball; but once I figured out what was going on, I actually savored the pleasure.

I reread the "high high . . . low low" sentence twice; stumbled; but liked it too. A kind of squeezed together sentence.

I stopped with "tip off." For a moment I didn't know what it was and then remembered/figured it out.

I was most caught up in the paragraph with all the sounds: I wasn't aware of my reading, got completely involved. I actually started to experience that large sound broken down into partial sounds.

I stumbled with the sentence about Washington getting the basket.

I think I am somehow bothered by the scoring business. Somehow I feel the writer (or the other fans?) taking it so seriously, but yet I feel at a distance from it; or I resist it. Partly I want to say, "Who cares." I don't know what makes me do that.

But somehow this combined with a general feeling of letdown in the last two paragraphs. I don't know where it's going—what it's about—I want more. I've liked reading this, but now it's slipping through my fingers. Somehow I become resistant as a reader in the next-to-last paragraph—and genuinely resistant in the last paragraph: I don't as it were "believe" that last paragraph.

Another Reader

The first sentence made me wonder why "Of course." Are you annoyed at always being early and having to wait too long for the game to start? Or do you deliberately come early to be a part of what's going on? Oh, Lord, this

is going to be about rooting for a team; those things are usually silly, immature babblings—I don't like it. I feel myself pulling away a little.

How can they block off half a court—I can't see it and I'm tempted to
start skimming stuff because I guess I want to see and can't.

For a minute I didn't realize you were describing basketball. Is she? I
asked myself and when I saw the bit about the tangled rope I knew you were.
Makes me see you as making fun of it, but that doesn't exactly fit in with
the previous stuff—so I feel a bit confused. Goals seem trivial to me: just
hoping to have more points after forty minutes. Then "tough" seems like
parody—hardly a thing to say about something like this. I find myself saying, "Oh, come off it!" But the end of the paragraph wins me over a bit
because the wording is so precise—one of those phrases where all the words
work.

"Finally"—was it a long time? Didn't really seem like it to me—just
because you say it is doesn't make me believe it. A little phony. Color is
wonderful, and here I feel some excitement and get pulled in—it's straight,
not corny—real.

Exclamation point doesn't work for me—maybe the way it's phrased
("It's also the first point of the game!") Again, I get caught up (against my
will?) by the remarks isolated out of the general noise; I'm beginning to
believe this is not a typical great-fun-at-the-game story. Cognitively interesting: the bit about fans thinking players actually hear them. Does a team
hear what we say? Do we think they do? Single voices blending back into
generalized noise—get the sensation of separate colors blending into one.
It's nice that it isn't overstated.

Attempt at suspense again to describe end of first half—I don't feel it,
just know it exists for others. Feel sort of embarrassed for you that you're
trying and not succeeding, overplaying a bit. But with rising temperatures I
get a physical sensation of heat, and I do begin to believe in excitement and
suspense. Exclamation point works better for me here. Hysteria after that: I
feel a break of the tension, so I guess I must have been feeling some tension.

I feel some calmness during half time and yet maintenance of some
tension. "Cold cement" sort of surprised me; I think I was still feeling
warm—so it hit a bit like a shock since I know what it feels like to sit unex-
pectedly on cold cement.

Nice coming back to just the speaker; I'd almost forgot about you. You
strike me as an island of calm, and that makes it feel like an ending.

How a Writer Might Think about This Feedback

I like my first sentence; I don't think I care which way a reader might take
it. It could be either, although I guess we always got there early because we
did want to be a part of the pregame excitement. Maybe the first paragraph
is a bit long, but the confusion is part of what I want to get across.

And yes, my feelings are ambivalent, but basically I think it's okay to be a fan and cheer and all that. Maybe I worked too hard at the suspense in places—and since that isn't my main point, maybe I could do it some other way. But there does have to be some suspense, some caring about the scoring and what's going on. After all, that's why we're all there.

There are a few spots where I could change the wording, I guess, but what I really need to figure out is what I want to do with this piece—exactly what I want it to be. I really don't know what to do with the last sentence—I sort of liked it. Maybe I just need to do something about the last two paragraphs; that seems to be where the main problems are.

Sample Movies of the Reader's Mind (IV) for "Cleaning Up the Environment"

One Reader

I started off browsing through the paper, not really reading it, yet was predisposed to be a sympathetic reader. For I agree with the writer's feelings about the problem of trash and the environment. And I like the idea of someone writing something that's trying to *do* something about a real problem: writing as trying to affect the world.

But when I started actually reading, I was put off by the first sentence—"I think it's disgusting." Feels too much like just grousing, not really doing anything. Doesn't feel like the decisiveness I was wanting. But still I want to go with him.

I agree at the beginning of the second paragraph. But I start to feel a scolding tone which puts me off again somewhat.

I'm pulled into the canoe story (though I want a new paragraph there).

I'm beginning to notice the interjections of different language—more formal (and seemingly awkward), "essayish" language: "of a certain radius," "There is definitely a need," "These above statements are of how things are. . . ." But I find I read the piece as a draft, and instead of getting bothered I say, "This is a problem and he's got to work it out, but this is what comes of writing fast and trying to get it all down." That is, I don't like that stiff language, but somehow I'm not bothered or annoyed. In fact then I get interested in a thought that occurs to me: that this essay is coming from two different impulses—the impulse to write from the gut or from feelings and the impulse to be controlled and judicious. *I'm* always trying to reconcile those two in my writing too.

I love the story of the dorm room: the reality of it, the inevitability of it. A microcosm of the world. And I like how he doesn't seem so scolding. I think in a way he is idealistic—and yet in the last analysis what he says seems true: that if the roommate *really* knew and felt how much it bothered the others he wouldn't do it so much.

"Some of my opponents. . . ." I feel put off by this paragraph. It feels as though some teacher told him, "Stick in a paragraph about opposing arguments," and he is just going through the motions. I'm annoyed because he doesn't really seem to take it seriously—take opponents or other views seriously. It feels mechanical to me. (And in fact I have trouble following his language here.) Really those are serious objections, yet he doesn't really give *any* answer to them.

I continue bothered with the last two paragraphs. The one suggesting options seems so thin. Was he just tired and bored? Can the problem be solved with just money? And I can't understand the difference between sentences two and three. *I* think things *can* be done, but the writer won't give me enough help on it.

The last paragraph confirms my feeling that he was getting tired and bored. Sticking in the bit about animals—out of the blue, undeveloped. I happen to think that legislation can do a lot for this problem—but somehow the way he says it ("discussed between legislatures") makes it sound like an impossible idea. *Whereas* to have the suite mates discuss their problem— that seems possible and promising. Maybe the essential paper is really a local and personal one—only about him and his dorm situation. Is that the strength of it?

I guess in the end I'm feeling somewhat battered from dissatisfactions, but I'm essentially rooting for the piece and wanting him to make it strong: hoping he can save it from mere scolding or "venting"—and from weak writing—and give it the strength—of feeling *and* thinking—that I want it to have. I *don't* want to have it just turn into a personal story about his dorm situation: I am rooting for his impulse to deal with the issue on a wider front—a wider, stronger, more thought-through case. I'm hungry for action in the world.

Another Reader

Beginning seems a bit immature, but actually I agree with him, and I might say it the same way. Yeah, but people don't make the effort, so why make it sound as though it's nothing; that's exactly what people won't do. As an ex-cigarette smoker, I felt a bit guilty about that. Story about campground seems anticlimactic until I read the part about suggested solutions; the brother is really right on! Almost seems like essay starts over with the bit about the dorm room. I'm sensing anger—real anger. Seems like emotional blurting.

I see this is following usual suggestion to take notice of opponent's argument, but just seems like more anger. Do *I* live in a high-priced neighborhood—probably. Is it clean? Well, our block is, but the shopping area is disgusting. (See, I used the same word.) I see some attempt to continually connect big issue and small issue—I guess I sort of like that—bringing it down to such a personal level.

Yes, concerned citizens should do something.

The business about the animals seems incomplete and not very effective with me. And last sentence seems weak; I feel myself wanting more.

But the anger is appropriate; makes me angry too—wish more people were angry, but I'm not sure I'm very convinced by all this—wish the anger were channeled more—too much emotion and not enough reason. The part about the campground remains with me most strongly, although the business about the dorm room is obviously deeply felt.

V

Criterion-Based or Judgment-Based Responding

You will have noticed how we keep arguing that judgment is not the most useful and important feedback you can get—especially because you can't *trust* judgments about something as complicated as writing. But if we have succeeded in persuading you to distrust judgments and to learn and use the *other* kinds of feedback, then we are happy now to turn around and try to show you how to make judgments about writing a *bit* more trustworthy.

If you get *just one overall judgment* about a piece of writing (such as "B+" or "very weak" or "75"), you are getting the least trustworthy kind of verdict—and you don't learn much from it. That is, different readers come up with different overall judgments or grades because they reflect different criteria: some readers count more for originality of the ideas, others for organization, others for clarity, still others for grammar and spelling.

But if you can get readers to make individual judgments about *specific criteria* (such as clarity of language, clarity of organization, mechanics), then those judgments tend to be more trustworthy. Readers are more likely to agree about clarity of language than about the grade for the paper as a whole. In addition, of course, these more specific judgments teach you more.

The criteria that are traditionally applied to *imaginative* or *creative* writing are these:

- Description, vividness of details. (Do we experience what's there?)

- Character. (Do we find characters real or interesting?)

53

- Plot. (Is it a believable, interesting, or meaningful story?)

- Language. (Not just "Is it clear?" but "Is it alive and resonant with meaning?"—perhaps through imagery and metaphor.)

- Meaning; "So what?" (Is there a meaning or impact that makes it seem important or worthwhile?)

The criteria that are traditionally applied to *expository* writing, essays, or nonfiction are these:

- Focus on task. (If the piece is written in response to a question, task, or assignment, does it squarely *address* that question or task?)

- Content. Sometimes this single criterion is divided:

  — Ideas. Are there good ideas, insights, or a good understanding of the subject?

  — Details, support. Are the ideas supported enough with examples, evidence, details?

  — Reasoning. Is the reasoning valid or persuasive?

- Clarity. Are words, phrases, and sentences clear?

- Organization. Does it hang together well? Can readers follow easily?

- Sense of the writer. Is there a sense of engagement or commitment to the topic and an appropriate voice and stance toward the reader?

- Mechanics. Spelling, grammar, punctuation; proofreading.

But of course you needn't be bound by these. Perhaps the piece of writing itself suggests certain of its own criteria (for example, the main job might be to *convey information*). Or perhaps there are certain criteria *you* feel shaky about and want to work on (for example, *organization* or whether the *voice* sounds natural or fake). Or you can let readers specify the criteria that they find most important (for example, certain readers always like to comment on *paragraphing*).

You can use criteria in a somewhat quantitative way if you wish, in order to give a quick picture of the strengths and weaknesses of a piece of writing. That is, you could just ask readers to give a one-word judgment about each criterion (or perhaps just rate them strong, satisfactory, or weak—"+," "ok," "−"). They can do this very quickly, and thereby give you a snapshot of their opinion of strengths and weaknesses. This leaves them lots of time for what we would call more interesting and more *writerly* kinds of feedback.

Watch out though. There is something very seductive about quantitative *ratings* of writing. You can get preoccupied with judgment—become a "judgment junkie" or a "grade hound." And the judgers can get all caught up too and waste lots of time having arguments about whether the organization is, say, "weak" or "okay." We want you to spend some time learning to make these judgments—learning to give criterion-based feedback—so you know how to do it more responsibly than it is usually done. But once you have practiced all the kinds of feedback we suggest, don't forget to ask yourself *"What kind of feedback will really help me most in my writing?"* Don't assume that just because you are in the habit of getting judgments or grades (because of the way schools work) that this is the kind of feedback that will help your writing most. We find that movies of the reader's mind are usually more writerly and helpful.

Giving feedback to yourself. If you specify the criteria you want to know about, you gain a kind of leverage or perspective that helps you give feedback to yourself. Stating the criterion can focus your attention or help you see things you don't usually see in just reading over what you write. When you've written a draft and are about to read it over, you can pause and consciously ask yourself, "What criteria are most important for this piece of writing?" Or "What features of writing do I especially need to be careful about?" This will help you see more.

To readers:

You can make your criterion-based responses more valuable in two ways.

- Be specific: point to particular passages and words which lead you to the judgments you make.

- Be honest and try to give the writer the movies of your mind that lie *behind* these judgments. That is, what reactions *in you* led you to these judgments about, say, the organization? For example, if you felt the organization was poor, were you actually feeling lost as you read, or was the meaning perfectly clear to you but you noticed some backtracking? And in noticing it, were you annoyed or just sympathetically aware?

ooooo

Sample Criterion-Based Feedback (V) on "An Orange Basketball Game"

One Reader

- *Description, Vividness of Details.* Strong. Especially the sounds and smells.

- *Character.* Okay or strong. There is a strong presence and voice of the writer or narrator. And I get intrigued with her.

55

- *Language, Clarity.* Fairly strong. I find it lively and plain—and at times vivid. Some good images.

- *Meaning: So What?* Weak. I'm left hungry at the end knowing what to make of it all.

- *Insights, Understanding.* Okay. In a way I feel it as an analysis of a sports situation and get good insights. But I want more too.

- *Organization.* Okay, I guess. I was never troubled as I read, but at the end, not understanding the main focus or "so what?" I ended up worrying about the long first paragraph, and wondering what the "center" of the piece really is or should be.

- *Sense of the Writer.* Strong in a good way—because of the voice and character of narrator.

Another Reader

- *Focus on Task.* Good. Actual game stays subordinate to crowd excitement.

- *Description.* Strong, especially building up of sounds during play of first half.

- *Character.* Fans are believable, but I'm not sure about writer and her interest in game. I do feel she's a people person.

- *Plot.* Chronological, but places where it stops a bit are good. Not finishing game is okay.

- *Language.* Sometimes it's a bit too formal: "But they hope for the elation of winning"; "Wait with extreme anticipation." But one place it really works: "What a clamor!" I'm not sure about the tongue-in-cheek description of game. I have trouble judging it because it doesn't recur. Everything is very clear though. And I like "the high is much higher than the low is low." And I like all the orangeness.

- *Meaning.* The "So what?" comes through to me at the end stronger because the writer *doesn't* say how the game turns out. The meaning for me is: It's fun just to experience this; there doesn't have to be anything more than a feeling of oneness with people; it's okay to do that once in a while.

- *Idea or Content*

  — Insight, understanding: I particularly like the comment that fans think players can hear each one of them. I think the rendering of crowd psychology is valid.

  — Thinking, reasoning: not much emphasis on this, but that's okay.

PROCESS BOX

It's a Saturday morning in August. My wife is sleeping late. My kids are downstairs watching TV and playing computer games, and I'm upstairs in my study revising our textbook. Or rather I'm reading over the extensive reactions and comments on the draft of our textbook by four professional readers that Random House provided—to give us feedback for our revising.

I've been working on revising for three or four weeks, and I'm curious why it's taken me this long to really sit down and read through all the readers' comments all at once. Why have I been putting it off? A good question for process writing.

I start to make a few notes by hand—sitting in the easy chair where I'm reading—and then realize I should go over to the word processor and do a real piece of process writing. And as I start, it also strikes me that many student readers of our text won't be familiar with the feedback and editing procedure behind the publishing of a textbook. (I wasn't familiar with them till this project.) So let me back up a bit and turn this into a long process box and try to give a picture of some of these goings on.

Background to This Morning

On the basis of our proposal for a textbook (a full description of our project with a draft of the first unit—about 25 pages long) we worked out a contract with Random House to publish it. Our conversations were with the person who was to be our editor there, Steve Pensinger. When he got our good-but-not-final draft of the whole text, he sent it out to four readers to comment. (That was more than a year after our proposal.)

Of course, we read their comments carefully when we first received them from Pensinger five or six months ago. We didn't get them all at once but in three installments—as he got them from the readers. They were informal statements, but extensive: each from five to fifteen single-spaced pages long. They were addressed to Pensinger but seemed intended also for us—frankly telling what they considered good and not good in our draft.

We'd gotten reactions from a few friends and from a number of teachers who work with us in the Stony Brook Writing Program—and from the students of these teachers. But these comments from outside readers were special because they were the first ones from people we didn't know. If they were very negative it would have been scary. It's not that Random House could have backed out of publishing our book; they'd already agreed to publish it, and they are obliged to do it so long as we produce something close to what we'd promised. But if the reviews were very negative, we feared the editor could have put strong pressure on us to make changes we didn't want to make—even to make a different kind of textbook from what we had in mind.

We happened to know who one reader was because he was a friend and very sharp reader whom *we* had suggested. But otherwise these were anonymous. It's common for editors to remove the names of reviewers when passing on comments to authors—so reviewers feel freer about being honest. I always feel odd, somewhat bothered, reading anonymous comments. Nevertheless we felt pleased and lucky to have such extensive and careful feedback. You could say that the publisher went to the trouble to *hire* a little peer feedback group for Pat and me (for these readers are paid a fee).

One reader was definitely negative. He (he *seemed* male) thinks that our whole approach is a bit misguided or extreme, and he is clearly irritated by much or even most of what we do. But I don't feel threatened about his reactions because he made it clear that *his* premises for the teaching of writing are different from ours. Thus we're not writing a book for someone like him. (Of course, it would be nice if our draft had completely "converted" him to our way of teaching, but that's not the way things work.) The other three readers were really very respectful and much more positive than not. They pointed out some weaknesses and problems. But they did so in a gracious, friendly way—showing that they value our work. And most of all, they were *right* in their criticisms and *helpful* in their suggestions. Or so it seemed to us after we read them and talked it over between us.

They all agreed that our draft was much too long—indeed long-winded and talky. We were asking students to read too much of our explaining (and even preaching) of theory. This agreement on the part of all readers encouraged us to do some heavy cutting and tightening—and led us to dream up a structural feature we're very pleased with: the "Ruminations and Theory" sections at the end of most units for students to *skip* unless they're interested in our background thinking.

Also we'd had trouble meeting our first deadline, so our draft was really a bit careless—not even well proofread for mistakes in mechanics, spelling, and typing. To have this pointed out by professional readers was a bit embarrassing, but not lethal. It was clearly a draft—and we knew we'd work hard at cleaning up for the final draft. Also the publisher's copy editor would catch anything we miss.

This August Morning

But somehow it's not till this morning—and I'm almost half way through my revising work—that I sit down and read all four readers' comments again—all together with an eye to using them explicitly for revising. (Indeed, perhaps I am stopping to do this process writing in order to find yet another way to put off my "duty" of listening to feedback on our writing.)

I wonder what's been holding me back? Is it that I'm plain reluctant to hear feedback on my writing? I usually love getting it. And it's not that their feedback is particularly negative or irritating or in some way bothersome. Even the negative one doesn't bother me.

In a way I feel I've *already* learned from their feedback. I've thought a lot about it, and Pat and I have discussed their reactions and suggestions many times. Yet I must acknowledge that they wrote *lots* of small specific comments and suggestions that I couldn't possibly remember from my earlier reading—however careful. I'm really not sure why I haven't sat down to reread. I just detect a kind of stubborn resistance.

ooooo

There. I put aside this process writing and sat down and read them all. ("There now. That didn't taste so bad did it?") They really are very good, very helpful. I'm grateful to them—and to the editor for getting them. It's a pleasure to read someone taking one's work seriously and giving good suggestions. I've already benefited from them and will benefit more. (Some of them *might* feel we haven't followed all their suggestions, but of course the basic principle of feedback is clear: they get to say whatever they want—and we can't quarrel with their reactions. But we get to decide how to respond to their reactions and which suggestions to follow.)

And yet still, if I am honest, I must come back to recognizing that feeling: that reluctance to read them. I can't come up with any particular or interesting reason at this point. Perhaps it's just the basic human resistance to having to be corrected. (For example, since childhood I've hated it when people tell me to speak more slowly and clearly.) People tell me I'm good about listening to feedback and even going along with much of it—but perhaps my conscientiousness about it has allowed me to begin to notice that some part of me doesn't want it. Back to that primal feeling again: if only one could just do one's best writing and have it be loved as it is—and not *need* any feedback and revision.

PETER ELBOW, 8/87

- *Clarity.* Fine.

- *Organization.* No problems moving from point to point.

- *Sense of the Writer.* An infectious sense of excitement and involvement. At times it seems detached: spots where formality creeps in. A mixture of detachment and involvement and then the touch of irony.

- *Mechanics.* Good.

Sample Criterion-Based Feedback (V) on "Cleaning Up the Environment"

One Reader

- *Focus on Task.* I don't know if it is written in response to a set task or not.

- *Ideas or Content*
  (a) Insights, understanding. Okay. Some good ideas and insights here. I like his mind ranging across the different dimensions of the problem.
  (b) Thinking, reasoning. Weak. Very little reasoning at all. Mostly just the expressing of feelings or the asserting of appeals to common sense—but not backed up.

- *Clarity: Words, Phrases, and Sentences.* Mostly clear but two notably unclear places—for me—in the third and fourth paragraphs.

- *Organization.* If I diagram it or take an overall view of the scheme, it's very clearly organized: starts with the main assertion, then two examples, then objections, then proposals, and then the closing. (Though the injection of the animal issue at the end seems very random.) Nevertheless, I don't *experience* it as well organized. Somehow I bounce around and don't feel a clean overall scheme. The *realization* of the scheme seems obscured.

- *Sense of the Writer.* I like the strong feelings, but still the voice or stance needs work because (1) it drifts over into scolding, and (2) there is an uncomfortable mixture of casual and formal (and occasionally awkward) "essay" language.

Another Reader

- *Focus on Task.* Not sure what the task is—sometimes it seems just a release of emotion. Not sure what I'm to be persuaded of—that people are slobs? But I know that. Focus shifts for me.

- *Ideas or Content*
  - (a) Insight, understanding. See very little of this—very little attempt to understand litterbugs—even roommate.
  - (b) Thinking, reasoning. This is weakest of all, especially where he takes up possible opposing argument; he doesn't really deal with the costs or why costs would be worth it. Reasoning about animals seems strange: why should I care about animals cleaning up their own environment? And besides, I think some animals do.

- *Organization.* Connections between general and specific not always good: too abrupt and not made explicit. Doesn't seem to come to any conclusion. Mention of animals doesn't fit in. Actually, I don't see any pattern in the organization—or at least very little.

- *Sense of the Writer.* Voice is indignant, angry; tone is emotional and keeps argument from making points on the basis of logic. Seems at places like a long blurt with a few sort of reasonable sentences which are not followed up on (the opposing arguments, the cost, the animals).

- *Mechanics.* Paragraphing bothers me a bit. First paragraph in particular leaves me a bit breathless and wondering why all the examples are in one long second paragraph. But basically the mechanics are correct.

- *Language.* Sounds adolescent—probably because of high number of emotional words.

Summary of Ways of Responding

THE TWO PARADOXES OF RESPONDING

First paradox: The reader is always right; the writer is always right.

The reader gets to decide what's true about her reaction: about what she sees or what happened to her, about what she thinks or how she feels. It makes no sense to quarrel with the reader about what's happening to her (though you can ask the reader to explain more fully what she is saying).

But you, as the writer, get to decide what to do about the feedback you get: what changes to make, if any. You don't have to follow her advice. Just listen openly—swallow it all. You can do that better if you realize that you get to take your time and make up your own mind—perhaps making no changes in your writing at all.

Second paradox: The writer must be in charge; the writer must sit back quietly too.

As the writer, you must be in control. It's your writing. Don't be passive or helpless. Don't just put your writing out and let them give you *any* feedback. You need to decide what kind of feedback (if any) you need for this particular piece of writing. Is your main goal to improve this piece of writing? Or perhaps you don't really care about working any more on this piece—your main goal is to work on your writing in general. Or perhaps you don't want to *work* at anything—but instead just enjoy sharing this piece and hearing what others have to say. You need to make your own decision about what kind of feedback will help you. Don't let readers make those decisions.

Therefore ask readers for what you want or need—and insist that you get it. Don't be afraid to stop them if they start giving you what you don't want. (Remember, for instance, that even after you are very experienced with all kinds of feedback, you may need to ask readers to hold back *all criticism* for a piece that you feel tender about. This can be a very appropriate decision; stick up for it.)

Nevertheless, you mostly have to sit back and just listen. If you are talking a lot, you are probably preventing them from giving you the good feedback they could give. (For example, don't argue if they misunderstand what you wrote. Their misunderstanding is valuable. You need to *understand* their misunderstanding better in order to figure out whether you need to make any changes.)

Let the readers tell you if they think you are asking for inappropriate feedback—or for feedback they can't give or don't want to give. For example, they may sense that your piece is still unformed and think that it doesn't make sense to give judgment. They may think sayback or descriptive feedback would be more helpful. Or they may simply hate giving judgment. Listen to them. See whether perhaps you should go along: they may be right.

If you aren't getting honest, serious, or caring feedback, don't just blame your readers. It's probably because you haven't convinced them that you really want it. Instead of *blaming* the readers, simply *insist that they give you what you need.*

What follows is a summary of the kinds of feedback we have earlier described.

I. NO RESPONDING: SHARING

How to Use It	*When It's Useful*
Just read your words out loud; see what they sound like. You probably learn more from the act of *reading in the presence of listeners* than from any kind of feedback.	When you don't have much time. Or at a very early stage when you're just exploring or feeling fragile about what you've written and don't want criticism. It's also useful when you are completely finished with a piece: you've finally got it the way you want it or you don't have the time or energy to make any changes—so it's time to celebrate by *sharing* it with others and not getting feedback at all.

II. DESCRIPTIVE RESPONDING

Sayback

How to Use It	When It's Useful
Ask readers: "Say back to me in your own words what you hear me getting at in my writing. But say it more as a question than as an answer—to invite me to figure out better what I *really* want to say."	At an early stage when you are still groping, when you may not yet have been able to write what you are really trying to say. If readers say back to you what they hear—and invite you to talk—this often leads you to *exactly* what you want to write.

Pointing

How to Use It	When It's Useful
Ask readers: "Which words or phrases stick in mind? Which passages or features did you like best? Don't explain why."	When you want to know what is getting through. Or when you want a bit of confidence and support.

Summarizing

How to Use It	When It's Useful
Ask: "What do you hear as my main point or idea (or event or feeling)? And the subsidiary ones?"	When you want to know what's getting through. If a reader says she disagrees with you, you need to know what she thinks you are saying.

What's Almost Said or Implied

How to Use It	When It's Useful
Ask readers: "What's *almost* said, implied, hovering around the edges? What would you like to hear more about?"	When you need new ideas or need to expand or develop what you've written—or when you feel your piece isn't rich or interesting enough. What you *don't* say in a piece of writing often determines the reactions of readers as much as what you do say. If this is an important piece of writing for you, you had better look to feedback about the implications.

Center of Gravity

How to Use It	*When It's Useful*
Ask readers: "What do you sense as the source of energy, the focal point, the seedbed, the generative center for this piece?" (The center of gravity might well *not* be the "main point" but rather some image, phrase, quotation, detail, or example.)	Same as for "What's Almost Said," above.

Structure; Voice, Point of View, Attitude toward the Reader; Level of Abstraction or Concreteness; Language, Diction, Syntax

How to Use Them	*When They're Useful*
Ask readers to describe each of these features or dimensions of your writing.	At any stage. When you need more perspective.

Metaphorical Descriptions

How to Use Them	*When They're Useful*
Ask readers: "Describe my piece in terms of weathers, clothing, colors, animals. Describe the shape of my piece. Give me a picture of the reader-writer relationship. What's your fantasy of what was on my mind that I *wasn't* writing about ('substitute writing')?"	At any stage. When your writing feels stale and you need a fresh view. If readers learn to give this kind of feedback, their other feedback tends to improve. Sometimes young, inexperienced, or naive readers can't give you other kinds of feedback but give very perceptive metaphorical feedback.

III. ANALYTIC RESPONDING

Skeleton Feedback

How to Use It	*When It's Useful*
Ask readers to tell you about these three main dimensions of your paper: • Reasons and support. ("What do	When writing a persuasive essay or any essay that makes a claim. At an early stage when you have a lot of unorganized exploratory writing,

Skeleton Feedback (Continued)

How to Use It	When It's Useful
you see as my main point and my sub-points—and the arguments or evidence that I give or could give to support each?") • Assumptions. ("What does my paper seem to take for granted?") • Audience. ("Who do I imply as my audience? How would my reasons work for them? How do I seem to treat them in general?")	skeleton feedback is a way to get help from your readers in adding to and organizing your material. At a late stage, readers help you analyze strengths and weaknesses. It's also helpful for giving *yourself* feedback.

Believing and Doubting

How to Use It	When It's Useful
Ask readers: "Believe (or pretend to believe) everything I have written. Be my ally and tell me what you see. Give me more ideas and perceptions to help my case. Then doubt everything and tell me what you see. What arguments can be made against what I say?"	The believing game alone is good when you want help and support for an argument you are struggling with. Together they are useful at any stage. They provide strong perspective.

Descriptive Outline

How to Use It	When It's Useful
Ask readers: "Write me *says* and *does* sentences—for my whole essay and for each paragraph or section." *Does* sentences shouldn't mention the content of the paragraph—i.e., shouldn't slide into repeating the *says* sentences.	Descriptive outlines make most sense for essays—and are particularly useful for persuasive pieces or arguments. They give you the most *perspective.* Only feasible when the reader has the text in hand and can give a lot of time and care. Particularly useful for giving feedback to yourself.

IV. READER-BASED RESPONDING: MOVIES OF THE READER'S MIND

How to Use It	*When It's Useful*
Get readers to tell you frankly *what happens inside their heads* as they read your words. Here are ways to help them: • Interrupt their reading and have them tell their interim reactions. • Get them to tell reactions in the form of a story (first . . . then . . .). • Get them to give subjective "I statements" about what is happening in them, not allegedly objective "it statements" about the text. • If they are stuck, ask them questions (e.g., about where they go along and where they resist, about their feelings on the topic before and after reading).	Movies of the reader's mind are useful at any stage—but they depend on a relationship of trust and support with readers. They can lead to blunt criticism. They're most useful for long-range learning: they may not give you direct help in improving this particular draft.

V. CRITERION-BASED OR JUDGMENT-BASED RESPONDING

How to Use It	*When It's Useful*
Traditional criteria for imaginative or creative writing: • Description, vividness of details. (Do we *experience* what's there?) • Character. (Do we find characters real or interesting?) • Plot. (Is it believable, interesting, or meaningful?) • Language. (Not just "Is it clear?" but "Is it alive and resonant with meaning?"—perhaps through imagery and metaphor.)	When you want to know how your writing measures up to certain criteria. Or when you need a quick overview of strengths and weaknesses. This kind of feedback depends on experienced and skilled readers. And still you should always take it with a grain of salt.

67

How to Use It	*When It's Useful*

- Meaning; so what? (Is there a meaning or impact that makes it seem important or worthwhile?)

Traditional criteria for expository or essay writing:

- Focus on task. (Does it squarely *address* the assignment, question, or task?)
- Content. (You might want to distinguish three dimensions: ideas; details or examples; reasoning.)
- Clarity.
- Organization.
- Sense of the writer. (Voice, tone, stance toward the reader.)
- Mechanics. (Spelling, grammar, punctuation; proofreading.)

Of course, you can specify whatever criteria you think right for a given piece of writing: what the particular writing task demands (e.g., persuading the reader) or what you are currently working on (e.g., voice). Or you can let *readers* specify the criteria that they think are most important.

FEEDBACK FROM YOURSELF

Certain of these feedback procedures particularly increase your perspective and thus improve your feedback from yourself.

- Certain kinds of *descriptive feedback* sharpen your eye, help you see things about your text you hadn't noticed (e.g., summarizing; describing the structure; the voice and point of view; level of abstraction/concreteness; language, diction, syntax).
- *Descriptive outline* and *skeleton feedback* are particularly powerful analytic structures that help you see what's strong and weak in any essay.
- *Criterion-based feedback* can help you zero in on features you know

you need to be careful about, for example, "Is it organized?" "Enough details or examples?" "Quotation mark problems?"

- Don't forget that if you do *process writing* about what you have written, you will probably come up with helpful suggestions for yourself. Talk about what pleases you and where you are troubled; spell out your frustrations.